A TICKET OUT

From The Steelworks To The Black Stump

STEVE WOODS

Publish & Print
www.publishandprint.co.uk

For My Mother

Contents

Night Shift Spark

So that's the shift all done, no fun
on nights I'm mixed up, overdone.
The early hours awake I go
where machines break down or move too slow.

By 3am my mind bemused,
the novelty gone, I feel confused.
If I'm called now I know I'll struggle,
electrical faults require clarity not muddle.

Hand-over done, I can cut and run,
now bath-house shower, first signs of sun.
I'm weak and tired, and life's gone stale,
I've steelworks pallor, but I'm out of jail.

At last to bed I drop away,
my need to sleep will not delay.
Can this be normal, 21 years old,
life lived this way, should I be more bold?

The irony is, I feel I matter,
a youngster needs that on his platter.
Although it's hard, I'm satisfied
when work machines, that I untied.

I sleep too deep to dream alas,
I'd love to form a plan to pass
from this strange world, nocturnal drift,
but not today, it's my next shift.

One day in the life of a steelworks spark

I

14:00 hours. "Here we go again John. Where's Andy?" Andy is just 16 and an electrical apprentice in our workshop. When he disappears we know why: He's unloading the 'male burden', a copy of a girlie mag in hand. "In the toilet block," Phil said. He'll have his leg pulled of course, but nature, not nurture is key with hormones.

"Am I floating?" The three sparks on D shift covered the whole steel plant. One up the steelworks, one down the sheet works and myself, normally the floater at this time. Two 'mates' supported us. The floater usually works alone. "Yes Steve. John will cover the sheet works as usual." Jack the foreman said. "Phil will take Andy and do some Kalamazoo (planned preventative maintenance, or PPM) until 4:30, when Andy goes home." Apprentices only worked day shifts.

We worked a three shift 'continental pattern' covering the works 24/7. Two morning shifts (6-2), then two afternoon shifts (2-10) and finally two night shifts (10-6). Whatever you worked on a Friday, you also worked on the following Saturday and Sunday. There were day shift electricians (8-4:30), who carried out most of the Kalamazoo. All workshop personnel, except apprentices, worked weekends in their respective shift patterns.

The 2-10 shift was my favourite. My worst was nights and, as a male in my early 20's, I wasn't too clever in the mornings. But I made it – just. I tended to burn the candle at all three ends. I had a busy life – girlfriends, football (too small for rugby), pub social life etc. The usual mix in South Wales, if you're lucky. I felt I was.

I liked floating. The work was always interesting. I loved fault finding. Being an industrial electrician opens up the satisfaction of engaging in a kind of detective work. It's almost addictive. It also meant I was peripatetic – entitled to go anywhere in the entire plant. Some of the older men preferred regular day shifts. They were always home every evening at a 'sensible' time. This was no good to me as it would mean Kalamazoo, a repetitive but necessary job; but then, so is cleaning the sewers! No, I liked the challenge of bringing reluctant machinery and plant back to life, keeping everything running. I felt I was a good fit for my work.

The other two sparks on D shift, along with Sid and Brian (the mates) moved out towards their respective territories. The electrical workshop was central to the whole plant, a stainless and special steels business at the time. About a mile long from north to south and perhaps 300yards wide. I was in the workshop alone, while Jack was in the foreman's office drinking his Earl Grey tea. Really pungent peppermint smells emitted from the open door. I don't know how he could put milk in it, but he did.

Jack was old school. These types came out of the war and early post war years, gaining skills and obtaining 'grace' to practice as electricians by employers and engineers desperate for skilled manpower to fuel the 1960's manufacturing boom. Jack was one of these and he was smart. I found that all these guys had good memories. They tended to remember a catalogue of faults and situations so they could find a solution. Invaluable stuff, but if a problem came up without a memory cover, they would pull in the younger generation, trained in the modern way.

I was trained over four years to be an electrician. This was formal, behind the desk stuff, carried out one or two days a week in a Pontypool Technical College. It was complemented through the rest of the week by working on the plant, alongside some very clever people. A lot can rub off onto a young boy (it was all male in those days), both good and bad. I learned a lot, and fast. I can recall my first pay packet; I got £4.10shillings. After a few weeks, it went up to £5.00, as I had finished paying for my steel toe-capped safety boots!

Due to lack of experience, our generation were obliged to be more analytical in our fault finding. Check the electrical schematic drawings, consult the machine operators (very important), do some tests and arrive logically at the cause of the fault. There was a saying in the steel plant world: an electrician will spend a day finding the fault and ten minutes to put it right. A fitter (there were many mechanical fitters in any steel works) would find the problem straight away; for example, a wheel off a gantry crane is an easy fault to find, but it takes all day to fix. I liked the electrical way.

I respected Jack. You can usually tell if someone is worthy of respect in the steel works world. He was. He was also very patient with me, especially on nights, when I struggled to keep awake. He would call upstairs, "Steve – number three pickle line is down, go and take a look." No answer – "Steve," more urgently this time. I knew I had to get down the metal stairway from the mess before the third call. I don't know how I never fell down those stairs!

The shift had settled down by now. My tool bag was on my workbench, ready for a call. It was always a shoulder bag, so we could ascend the gantries and other metalworks to attend to cranes etc., using both hands to climb. Most shift electricians carried a decent lantern type torch in their bag. Mine is a hand me down from a retired spark. After 5pm, or 17:00 hours in shift parlance, the office and day shift workers departed, leaving the plant, sort of, belonging to us.

We were kind of caretakers, it seemed to me. Most of my

fellow young sparks hated afternoon shifts. It interfered with their social activities. I felt that way early on, but later I had cooled just a bit and liked the atmosphere of the 2-10 shift. I also worked out that I got more Saturday afternoons off on shifts than on days – football! I would volunteer to cover 2-10 on A, B or C shift weekdays. Then, occasionally, I would ask for cover in return, for my night shifts. Nights paid the best, but I didn't care. I lived with my parents and my sister, so my income, apart from a small amount for my upkeep, was all mine.

Give and take worked well with our team. Again, I think this was handed down from the older guys as so much was, both regarding the job and life in general. Team work is essential in a steel works. It is a dangerous and hostile environment which punishes brutally those who ignore safety precautions, or sometimes innocents in the wrong place at the wrong time.

Occasionally we would hear of an injury or even a death somewhere on the plant. This was always regarded with much sadness, but accepted as a price to be paid. There was an 'it won't happen to me' attitude, which perhaps reflects the thinking of soldiers in combat. We seemed to be able to adapt to the reality of risk in life; probably no bad thing.

Most of us younger sparks had learned a lot about the fair sex at the hands of the old lags. Innocent 16-year-old apprentices, we would listen as they filled our heads, our imaginations, with pictures of a life which, seemingly, had long passed them by. We were still right in the centre of this hormonal morass. Unpredictable, often exciting, but never boring. The job is a bit like that. So it fits in with my age related enquiring mind. Amazing!

*

At 18:00, if it was quiet, we all sat down to tea and the evening meal together. We often played cards after tea. I looked forward to this. Sometimes it was 9 card Don – not my thing, but Phat is great; a team game like Bridge, only simpler. I think youngsters love team games. It's only when you're older that 'individuation' seems to get a grip.

I tended to gobble my food down, usually sandwiches lovingly made by my mother. We got tea using hot water from the urn and then – cards. I always ate fast for another reason; to avoid the smoke. My mother and father both smoked, my sister and I hated it. At tea in the mess room the window was always open. There was just one smoker on our shift, Brian. You ate to finish before him, so avoiding the noxious fumes affecting your appetite. I am quite fussy for a steelworks worker!

The mess room is an austere box set above the office. Down the middle is placed a long table covered with stainless sheet, and benches on either side. To brighten it up, some had put girlie pictures on the walls as was normal in such environments. I suppose to remind us all that fantasies matter even when humans inhabit such a dismal workplace.

With luck I'd get John as a playing partner for Phat. I looked up to John. At 35 he had the mind of an 18-year-old. Refreshing and entertaining, not given over to the shroud of responsibility. I didn't think John would ever grow up, even though he had a wife and three children! He was clever. Clever enough not to work too hard. By contrast, I thrived on work. I found his outlook fascinating. Out of luck today, it's Don. I sit back and watch.

Phil, the other spark, had more of a quiet disposition. A little younger than I, Phil was, nevertheless, ahead of his years regarding being responsible. He liked his bike, an Ariel of some kind, I think. Despite his biker image, I felt Phil would drop into married life very easily, when the time came. The two mates, Brian and Sid, were old school and did their jobs with little enthusiasm, merely as a means of earning a living. The job I did was much more than that to me.

I had a scooter when I was seventeen, to get me to and from work – and for fun! It was a cream coloured Vesper 180 SS. Since I had a scooter and not a bike, I was a 'mod' not a 'rocker'. My machine had a network of mirrors at the front, as was normal on scooters in the late sixties and early seventies. It was quite a powerful machine and I sometimes had to tow one of my mates' Lambretta's home after it broke down.

I well remember, on cold winter nights, we would get together and scoot off somewhere. We all had army surplus great coats to keep out the cold; mine was an RAF one. I was quite proud of it. I was knocked off my scooter one day returning from the Orb works apprentice training centre in Newport. I lost consciousness and woke up in hospital. I was lucky; I had my helmet on (this was not compulsory in those days) and I got away with it, but no more scooters! I got a Triumph herald instead. After several cars (including a mini which I smashed up – it's complicated), I finally got my lovely Rover 2000. Much more my thing.

It's quiet so I tell Jack I'm going to pop down the sheet works fitting shop. This is the main workshop for mechanical engineering in the works. It is based there because the technology in a sheet works is more sophisticated than in a steel plant. Rolling mills, Pickle lines and Bright Annealing lines are heavy-duty engineering. Where we had seven shift personnel, including the foreman, they had eight fitters and nearly as many mates, as well as two welders. This was due to their work being much more physical than ours.

It's a ten-minute walk down to the fitters workshop. The sheet works was made up of long bays, each with their two cranes to service the machinery below. A bit like Paddington or Victoria railway stations, in structure; I thought of them as Cathedrals of heavy industry. Passing through the shearers shop and the side trim and cut-up lines, I am reminded of something casually pointed out to me when I was shown around, as a first year apprentice: "Count the fingers on the operators' hands" I was told. I did so covertly and noticed that a few of the older operators did not possess a full set of digits. This made me cringe. The powerful and imposing shearing machines (guillotines really) would make short work of any skin and bone, which might lay in their path.

As I walked into the fitting shop, I noted that, unlike ours, it is a cold and inhospitable place. Just a draughty enclosure inside the larger sheet works area. By contrast, our shop is located handily opposite the carpenters shop and is a self-contained brick affair, with a door at the front and another at the rear. We can therefore keep it warm in the bitter winter weather. Not so the fitters shop. No amount of heat would make that place warm. There are huge gas heaters about their workshop to blast heat out into the machine area, where turners stand at their machines, freezing on one side and boiling on the other. I thank my lucky stars I chose an electrical and not mechanical apprenticeship.

I'm looking for Owen. He is a fitter; younger than me and already married. He had offered to make a pair of car ramps for my Rover. They needed to be of sturdy welded construction to take my car, which weighs nearly a ton. He is in the mess room drinking tea. "They're just about finished," he said. We go out into the workshop to take a look. "I'll drop them off at your place Saturday afternoon if you like." This suited us both as he was off and I was nights. This kind of 'job on the side' was, strictly speaking, not permitted.

You used both materials and labour, which belonged to the British Steel Corporation – the agglomeration made up when all the old privately owned steelworks were nationalised, under the Labour government.

The previous company owners of this works were the Richard, Thomas and Baldwin group, or RTB for short. Some of the old lags still referred to it as 'RTBs' or RT's. Old traditions still existed though. For instance, under an industrial relations policy known as 'sociability'[1] the former General Managers House in Griffithstown was given over as a works club. Panteg House has a cricket pitch, tennis courts and snooker tables as well as a bar and lounge, which were well used. All employees had equal use of these facilities. Benevolent patriarchal capitalism has its advantages!

While we chat, Owen mentions that he has applied for emigration to Australia. I am immediately envious. Here is this married tradesman, even younger than me, getting it together to see some of the world. "It's assisted passage," he said. This meant he wouldn't have to pay for his and his wife's flights, as long as he agreed to go to his sponsoring employer in New South Wales and stay there for a year. After that, he was free to go anywhere in Australia to work.

Wonderful. I couldn't think of anything more exciting. "When will you hear?" I asked. "Four weeks," he said. If successful they will have 'permanent resident' visas, which they must use within three months of acceptance, to go. When you consider where we were both standing at that moment, it seemed very exotic indeed! My head was in a whirl as I walked back up to the electrical workshop. Could I do this too?

Although I dreamt of one day travelling far, perhaps as far as Australia, I was in the here and now most of the time. As with many youngsters, there were two sides to my character. The side which wanted things to remain as they were, so I could continue enjoying my work and life; but also the side that was looking for change and adventure outside the world in which I lived. For the time being, the cautious side was uppermost.

*

It's dark now. Jack and I are alone again in the workshop. It seems I'm having a quiet shift, when the phone rings and Jack tells me to go up the melting shop (at the north end of the steelworks) and look at a fault on the 100-tonne crane. They are due to 'tap' the furnace in half an hour and they can't do it without that huge gantry crane. Phil and Sid are tied up on another job.

I pick up my bag. This is the part I love best. As I walked past the clocking-in station and up through the works, towards the Centro-maskin steel slab grinding bay, I recalled the old melting shop, located about where I am walking now. It consisted of three electric arc furnaces, 'S', 'T' and 'U'. I believe there was once an 'R', which had a capacity of 5-tons, while 'S', 'T' and 'U' were 10-tonners. They were pulled out a year into my apprenticeship to be replaced by the new melting shop with its 40-tonner in 1971.

Back in the present, I consider the fault. The-100 tonner will not lower the larger of its two hooks. Not much use if a crane can't lower its hook. It is one of the modern 3 phase AC types of crane, with power supplied by the three large electrical busbars going the full length of the melting shop. It is the biggest crane in the works.

I remembered the time in the sheet works when, on an old DC powered crane, I almost fried. I was a fourth year apprentice, sent down with a mate to replace a power line 'trolley wheel'. Rather like the old trolley buses, these transmit power from the two overhead wires, running the length of the shop, to the crane. I was on the crane, just about to grab the wheel and put it back on the wire when I hesitated. I will never know why, but instead I reached down into my bag, grabbed a large spanner and slapped it across the two wires. This is something sparks do if they think there may still be power on the lines. Fuck! I thought to myself in a sudden sweat. The spanner stuck! I had just saved my own life. The mate below, by the isolation switch, had misinterpreted my signal to switch off.

This, I feel, was just the sort of cultural 'sixth sense' that the experienced old lags had passed on to us youngsters. You can't learn that in trade school. I will always be grateful. Not long after, the Engineers set up a personal lock system. Each tradesman in the plant was issued with a long hafted padlock and a safety sign, with name, clock number and department etched into it. I still have mine to this day. A S Woods C/No 5 ED (Electrical Department). I'm sure this system saved lives. No one, not even the works manager, could remove one of these signs and padlocks. That was how safety could be guaranteed. On more than one occasion however, someone from works security had to drive to a tradesman's house and take him back to work to unlock the electrical switch he had forgotten he had locked off. (No, not me!)

Incidentally, the 'A' stands for Adrian. My parents wanted to name me Stephen, but my maternal grandmother liked Adrian. No problem, except it would have been S.A.Woods, SAW Woods! So they swapped it around, but I was always called Stephen; which is what I answer to.

The only time I can recall that I was injured, apart from minor cuts and grazes, was whilst working in the melting shop precipitator. This is a huge metal box with the function of removing metallic pollution from the air before release into the environment. It worked by the internal application of an electrostatic charge of electricity in a flood of spray water (hence the name precipitator).

Periodically, electricians and fitters were required to enter the box to check the apparatus and to clean the insides down respectively. The box had entry hatches that were heavy, rather like those found on a large ship. As I was passing through one of these, the catch failed and the lid fell on me. I was lucky. It could have easily broken a bone, but I just received a deepish cut at my right hip. Happily, the scar has faded over the years.

When I arrive at the furnace I consult the operators then walk to the access ladder and climb to the crane above, which is at least 70 feet up. I talk to the crane driver, Mike. The sulphur fumes and dust up here are thick and getting thicker as the electric arc furnace nears tapping time.

Looking down over the scene, I think how a non-steelworker might consider it. Dante's inferno comes to mind with the heat and flames bursting from the 40-tonne electric arc furnace, its three carbon electrodes probing down through the round chamber roof onto the molten high chromium steel below. The noise from the electric arcing is frighteningly loud. To the left, looking south, the great ingot jackets are lined up either side of a tapping funnel, up on the teeming platform. Everything is on an enormous scale in a steel works. From up high on a gantry crane, workers almost look like ants or, with the sulphur falling like snow, Zeks[2]. Men walk about in the grey half-light dressed in their fireproof clothing and safety hats. Yes, it looks like a version of hell!

As usual, I am methodical in my approach to the problem. I check the supply in the control panel tunnel, which spans the entire length of the crane, to make sure all three phases of the 440-volt electrical power are present. Although the tunnel lights are on, I need my torch for this. I have learned from hard experience not to assume the obvious; a little time spent early on usually saved a lot more later. I have some time, but not much. All this is thrilling when you are a young tradesman, confident about your job. I was at that stage. To me it had the spice of adventure about it.

Next I look to see if the appropriate electrical contactors and relays are energised and closed when Mike pushes the control leaver to 'lower'. Again, patiently studying the drawing pays off. The third stage contactor, although energised, is arcing. Poor contact. I look more closely; yes, this would do it. "Mike, stop lowering and turn the power off," I call.

Quickly cleaning the contactor with the appropriate emery paper I test for electrical continuity and brush the surrounding area clear of sulphur dust. Then, after powering up, Mike lowers – success. The tapping can go ahead and thousands of pounds worth of man-hours and materials are secure. Above all, this is deeply satisfying for me. First the puzzle, then the analysis, finally the outcome. Perfect! Definitely no other job could ever come near to such a trilogy.

I stay on the crane during the tapping, to be on hand should the problem reoccur; but also because I can't get off. There isn't time to take the crane back to the ladder access point. Mike suspends the huge ladle in the pit below the spout of the furnace. Slowly the furnace tilts forward on its hydraulically driven racks, so that the molten metal comes pouring from the furnace into the ladle. This is skilled teamwork between the furnace man and the crane driver. With the ladle full of molten metal, Mike swings it over to the Argon Oxygen Vessel for further refining. Down shop now, over the Vessel, he reverses the process using both hooks of the crane. The 100-tonne hook holds the ladle whilst the auxiliary smaller hook is used to raise its lower outer edge, rather like a teapot, so the metal pours into the waiting Vessel. Later, the metal will be tapped again and poured into the waiting casting moulds.

Crisis over, I descend the ladder heading for the charging cabin. This is the place to go for an illicit cup of tea. Phil and Sid are already there. I often think my long-term affection for a cuppa is due to the opportunities for refreshments in the steelworks! We saw it as reward for a job well done.

Sparks were always welcome in such cabins, which, because of the hostile work environment, were dotted about throughout the works. There was an implicit respect for us which I must admit I enjoyed, as any 23-year-old would. The charging area is where the different materials – stainless scrap such as old sink units, mild steel – you name it, along with raw minerals such as chromium and nickel are added to a furnace to obtain the correct mixture for the steel. A bit like a menu, the chef being the leading furnace hand. Always a very experienced man, He was the best paid hand in the steel plant. These men were tough dependable types, but they did not suffer fools gladly. They often took the mickey out of the younger more naive sparks and fitters, with calls to non-existent faults. I knew from experience they were testing us to see if we could 'take a ribbing'. All part of the rough and tumble steelworks social scene!

This testing out was especially prevalent with the first year apprentices. I well remember being told to go to the stores for a 'gear cutting chisel' by an older machinist. This was during the compulsory six months which apprentices of all disciplines served in the mechanical workshop. What's a gear cutting chisel? No such thing. Another popular gag was to instruct the apprentice to go to the stores for a 'long weight'. Of course, what the apprentice actually got was a long wait, sometimes very long, at the stores hatch. The storeman knowing exactly what was required!

*

Looking back, I wonder that I survived those first six months. Small, introverted and sensitive; none of these characteristics was desirable in the mechanical apprentice workshop. It was run by Richie Thomas, a clever good looking man who excelled at cricket (he played for the Panteg House eleven). Richie was quite strict and banged on to us about the correct and safest way to do things. I remember, on one occasion, we were not using the right technique with a hammer and chisel. Richie came out of his office and, after seizing the tools from a lad, proceeded to demonstrate the correct method. He then struck his own knuckles a nasty blow with the hammer. We all laughed and Richie retired to his office (sorry Richie).

The mechanical apprentices had to remain in the workshop for two years, I believe, to get the more detailed training in their field. The rest of us, electricians, instrument tech's and even a chemical engineering apprentice, all had just the six months to do.

Mike Davies (clock number 6) and I were the electrical contingent, while I remember Gareth Bessell was one of the fitters. (It was his Lambretta that I later towed with my Vespa scooter.) We heard through the grapevine that all first year lads would have to undergo an 'initiation' ceremony. Richie always seemed to disappear just before such ceremonies, as he could not be seen to condone such behaviour. There is not much doubt in my mind that this practice had been adopted from the public (fee paying) schools.

My fellow electrical apprentice, Mike, went through it first. He was a big lad, but he was clever enough not to resist. The older mechanical apprentices would suddenly rush the selected victim, then pin his arms by securing his overall sleeves in two vices on a work bench. Thus incapacitated, the victim would have green glutinous Swarfega (a kind of strong industrial soap) applied down the inside of his overalls and all over his head. Then, out came the sawdust, and this was liberally spread over the same areas. The first thing I thought was how uncomfortable it must be. I had heard that if you resisted, they put your head down the toilet to wash it off! So when my turn came, I did not resist. However, it didn't do my teenage acne any good! Glad to get it over though; as with most things you dread, the waiting was the worst.

Another tradition was for the first year boys to fetch the breakfast. We would take it in turns to go out of the main gate and over the road to the canteen, with an order list for baps and all round greasy food for the mid-morning break (in Australia they call this 'smoko'). I had a bit of a show down with one of these older boys, Steven Warfield if I recall correctly. The thing was, I refused to fetch cigarettes. I would never do it for my own mother and I was not going to do it for anyone else. Luckily, someone else volunteered to come with me and collect them. Crisis over. It has always been that way with me. If I get set in my mind about something, that is usually it.

In the apprentice mechanical workshop there was every type of machine for cutting, milling, shaping and drilling metal. Before we could touch a machine though, Richie taught us how to use basic tools. The very first job was to file a piece of mild steel until it was a one-inch cube. He allowed us a small tolerance (10 thousandths of an inch or so). Most of us spent nearly a week doing this. We were all very good at filing metal afterwards though! Later, we made a few hand tools, such as pipe grips and then we made our own toolboxes. We had basic training on the machines and that was it. We were out.

*

It's after 2100 hours now so Phil, Sid and I head back to the workshop to check for other jobs before handing over the works to the night shift. After reporting back to Jack, we hear that Jack Mansell won't be in for his night shift. This is grist to the mill for John. Jack Mansell usually takes the sheet works so John is offered a 'doubler'; that is, the option of working a further 8 hours. He accepts, knowing full well he will be given a grace period of one hour to leave the works for refreshments at 21:30. If a job comes in, we will handle it between us for that short time, even if one of us stops back until 2230 hours.

For John, 'refreshment' meant a pint and a pie up the British Legion club, a short walk up the road from the works entrance. Being an ex amateur rugby player, John liked his pint. Looking at him, there's not much doubt he played in the pack. With his broken nose, missing teeth and cauliflower ears, his head had obviously been at the heart of many a scrum! He's gone in a flash and I decide to join him, all being well, at 22:00. This is a nice unwind for me after a satisfying shift. I can take a shower in the bathhouse later. So up I went to meet John and Brian. These two were the mischief makers of the shift.

I well remember, on nights a year or so back, John and Brian told me to follow them to the railway yard on the east side of the works for some fun. I'm 22 years old; I'm going to follow aren't I! We ended up careering about the rails on two dumper trucks. These are tough vehicles, much tougher than humans. I pulled a muscle but I don't know if it was due to the rough ride or because I was laughing too much! Illicit? definitely, dangerous? probably; but memorable fun just the same.

Halfway through his 'first' pint, John tells us that his bungalow in Talywain is almost finished. It's an open secret that John has been 'borrowing' cement from the furnace brickies in the steelworks, to build his bungalow. In fact, he is known as 'Johnny concrete'. We cannot believe that the engineers don't know about it, but it is surprising what you can get away with, out of sight on the back shifts!

I should mention here that we didn't have managers, as such. A generic manager such as exists in the outside world would probably get someone killed. No, it had to be done by experienced and qualified engineers. Safety demanded it. Luckily for John, engineers worked days only. At the top of the electrical department tree was the only university-trained engineer among us. David Lee was a tall man with a dignified bearing such that, although he was quiet and softly spoken, he exuded authority. We all referred to him as Father (not to his face of course), which gives an indication of the respect we had for him. There was no way that he knew about John's 'borrowings'!

John and Brian had spent the evening working on the Sendzimir mill with the shift electrical technician, Eddie. Eddie was the brains of our shift and was equal to Jack in the pecking order. Jack didn't tell Eddie to take a look at something, he asked him to. I wanted to be doing what Eddie did one day. He was consulted for only the most technically interesting work, but I knew I wasn't ready. Also, there was only one electrical technician on each shift, so vacancies were rare. The last one was taken by Chris. Though younger than I, Chris had better qualifications and was ready for the challenge.

A Sendzimir or 'Z' mill is a cold rolling plant designed to reduce the gauge of coiled stainless steel to the required commercial dimension. Although a small reduction compared to hot rolling mills, because the material is stainless, it is very hard. Much pressure is therefore applied to the rollers (think of two cotton reels with a mangle between them). Although relatively old technology by this time, the 'Z' mill was our primary means of carrying out this process. The only other mill in the works capable of this was the even older Four High mill. As its name suggests there are four huge rollers vertically mounted instead of the 'cluster' arrangement on the 'Z' mill.

Whenever I was in the vicinity of the mills I was always intimidated by the thought of what those rollers could do to any living thing that gets too near. Some have; enough said. A machine shop was located between the two mills and there was almost always a roller being ground ready for use when required. Maintenance never ends in a steel works.

Our mills each had a large sub-station where all the electrical gear, motors and generators necessary to power and control the processes, were housed. In the sub-stations, there were long lines of AC and DC electrical panels, on which were mounted the contactors, relays and all the other gear necessary to control the mills. Connecting it all together was a network of wiring harnesses. All this would be overwhelming without the advantage of wiring and schematic electrical drawings to 'navigate' by. It was essential to master the interpretation of these drawings in order to understand the process and find faults or replace equipment etc.

Beneath all this, there was a warren of access tunnels, not unlike wartime bunkers, which were used for cables, as well as hydraulic and compressed air pipes. I am not the best in confined spaces, but the young can adapt and I did so. Also to be found down here, if you knew where to look, was a comfortable 'palliasse' or two; a few pieces of soft packing sponge carefully arranged for sleep, during periods when tradesmen preferred not to be found by their foremen! I never spent longer than I had to anywhere near the mills. There was always an unhealthy oil laden steamy atmosphere around them.

I mentioned to John about Owen, the young fitter applying to emigrate to Oz. He told me that he had an older brother, Patrick, who did the same thing some years ago. This had ended badly, as he died in a car accident over there. I felt for John. He was not given to emotional outbursts, this almost casual mention of his brothers tragedy was as close as he came. I knew he was a big family man. I made a mental note that, if I ever got across to Oz myself and was anywhere near, I would put flowers on his brother's grave for his mum.

10:30 already and my pint is finished (my one to John's two). Over to the bathhouse next. Each locker was steam heated to dry the used towels. I opened mine, number 5 of course. There is a particular smell, which needs to be washed off, in a steelworks. The melting shop is mostly sulphur, while the sheet works is a mixture of hydrofluoric acid (the pickling lines) and hydraulic oil (the mills). A welcome shower, change and into the Rover. I take my usual route across Station road and down past Cwmbran Town Centre.

The town centre was new in the sense that it was mostly built in the early 1960's. I think, however, that it will always be known as the 'New Town Centre' by locals. Language has a way of overtaking the original purpose of an expression, it is a living thing in that sense. The Rover almost knows its own way home by now.

This was my home town, I had never lived anywhere else, so I knew it well. I saw the Cwmbran Development Corporation change the landscape before my eyes as I grew up. This housing project was possible because the valley is 'U' shaped, and not 'V' shaped like most Welsh valleys. The people here tend to be from all over, which promotes a diversity not seen in other valleys. I park outside my parents 1930's semi-detached house (council house, that is) and enter through the back door as usual. No one up, bed.

*

I think about the day I have had; about Owen's potential adventure and John's brother, now buried in Perth, Western Australia, he said. Owen said that the Australians had a points system for emigration, which favoured married couples. I was a bit light on points at the time as I was 'between girlfriends'. The field was smaller for me than for most boys because I could never go out with a smoker. Something like 50 per cent of British girls in my age group smoked; a serious disadvantage for a young red-blooded male.

I note that I am already thinking 'strategically' about a possible new life abroad, but I have always been a dreamer, so my mind goes all over the place randomly sometimes. I imagine myself in all sorts of situations. One dream is to sail gently around the world in my own boat, visiting tropical places and meeting interesting people along the way. I never stay anywhere for too long in this dream, always moving on, over the horizon. This is my regular 'out of the box' adventure type dream. I was sure about one thing though, I had been born at Panteg hospital, I was working in Panteg Steel works and there was no way I would die in Panteg!

Tiring now, I listened to my music; mostly consisting of instrumental pieces by Tangerine Dream (Rubicon) and Jean Michel Jarre (Oxygene), as well as some Moody Blues. The Moody Blues album 'On the Threshold of a Dream' does just that and I sleep soundly. There was an old Danset record player in the corner of my room, but I only used it as a table and played my music on recorded cassettes. I was usually asleep before the end of the tape. I never had it too loud so my parents weren't disturbed.

It is interesting that young people love music. It seems to be the modern equivalent of poetry. For me, groups such as The Moody Blues definitely used poetic lyrics, delivered with the agency of their music. Such combinations must be among the most potent of influences on the young.

I had the smallest bedroom. My sister Julie was in the bigger one at the front of the house, with a double bed (luxury) and the nice warm airing cupboard. Mam and dad, of course, had the other double room. They shared an internal wall with me. Mine was the box room with a single bed and a built in wardrobe for my clothes (my dad's handiwork). I was happy with it though, as I was only in it to sleep.

The sun lights up the curtains at the window. I'm awakened and the time is 9:05am according to my alarm clock, which I always set 5 minutes fast to try and 'beat the clock' (the works one that is). Julie and dad would have gone to work already. I am a deep sleeper, so I heard nothing.

Dad was a postman and they get up in the mornings at 5am. The first job I can recall him doing was working in the GKN engine casting factory in old Cwmbran. It was heavy, dirty work. I remember as a child when he would pick me up, he had very rough hands, ingrained with the oily dirt of the GKN foundry. Much later on, GKN was one of two companies that offered me a place as an apprentice. After considering it, I turned it down. There is no doubt that my father's experience would have been a factor. All the more so, as I would have become a mechanical fitter. I was much more attracted to the electrical apprenticeship offered by Panteg. So that is how it turned out.

Later on, my father worked shifts for the Girlings car brakes firm, but had to finish as he just couldn't cope with nights.

Genetic then! His brother Arthur was in an office job with the post office and he 'got dad in'. It was how it was done in those days, across the social classes.

Julie worked as a clerk at the council offices in old Cwmbran. She is five years younger than I, so we were never in the same school at the same time. My sister was a much more confident child than I was and sometimes fought my battles for me out in the brutal pecking order of children's society. In fact, the signs of her strength of will were there from an early age. Born in our two-bed home, she would never settle in the cot at the foot of my parents bed, and often jerked the whole construction back and forth until she could reach the wallpaper – which she loved to strip from the wall!

Later, as a toddler, when Julie couldn't get her own way, she would go into a rage and her face would literally change colour, which frightened my mother so much that she gave in. One day my maternal grandmother witnessed this, and promptly told my mother to let her daughter burn the anger out – which she did. After the fuss, Julie came to her mam for a cwtch (a Welsh expression for a nice secure hug). All was well from then on. By contrast, I was a very contented child, considering my restless nature later in life.

There was just one further demonstration of rebelliousness from my little sister. She was five or six years old and mam had annoyed her in some way. Julie went straight upstairs and pulled out our small travel suitcase. Into this she put her favourite dolly and... all her knickers! Off she went, declaring that she was leaving (dad followed just out of sight). I think she must have realised she was hungry, because she turned around and came back. Mam said that at least she would have had a clean bum. (Yes I *did* ask Julie's permission to put that one in.)

Being much older and of the opposite sex, I have never felt like my sister and I had a lot in common. However, our relationship is solid and we knew we would always 'be there for each other' when mam and dad were gone. That was what our parents wanted. That is also what we wanted. I was now wondering how a life in Australia could affect that bond!

I've always been proud of the fact that I named her – well, almost. When I was in primary school there was a girl who used to give me piggybacks in the schoolyard. I was a skinny little runt and she was, well, big! Her name was Julianna and she took to me and I to her. So when my parents presented this bundle of joy to my five-year-old self and asked me what we should call her, out came Julianna! Not particularly liking that long out of fashion name and probably wishing they hadn't asked me, my parents came up with the shortened version. They put this to me. Julie it was.

*

After having breakfast and cleaning up, I had until 1pm to occupy myself. Then it was time to prepare for my final afternoon shift of the week. It was Thursday so it meant nights on Friday, Saturday and Sunday. Not the best weekend for me. I couldn't socialise up the pub because if I drank I wouldn't stay awake on nights! However, I would be able to play football this week. The kick off was set for 3 o'clock. Oops, I'd arranged for Owen to drop my ramps off at 2. I would have to ring and ask him to come at 1 o'clock instead.

I loved playing football. I am not big but I was quite fast and left footed, so I played left wing. I admired the skills of the Brazilian footballer Rivellino (he was also a left winger after all). I had a very good 'cross', so I was popular with the centre forwards in my club. The club under-18 team (of which I was a member) went to Aston Villa to play an out of season friendly against their youth team. We were hammered. I remember admiring how their coaching and organisation was excellent. They were young professionals and played like it. We recovered some dignity later however, when we all sat down for a meal and, being Welsh, many of us drank way too much!

I did have a trial for the Monmouthshire county team but the left winger on the other side had a great game whilst I could not find the ball. I also attended an open trial at Bristol City with my friend David Giles, but that also came to nothing. The problem with being a winger is that you can spend long periods waiting for the ball to come to you. Occasionally, I went and found it. Sometimes I played left-midfield for the club. That was great because, in the middle of the park, you get a lot more ball!

I enjoyed football so much partly because I contracted rheumatic fever as a ten year old. I just tried to get out of bed one morning and fell straight on the floor; my left knee would not hold my weight. I had not slept well and was sweating. After that, I could not engage in physical exercise for two years. A long time for a youngster. I remember with tenderness my time in the children's ward of a local hospital (Robinson Crusoe ward; adventure keeps popping up in my world). My mother was sitting beside me, holding her tears back, the doctors thinking I had something 'serious'. They put it down to the damp in our house; we moved shortly afterwards, to Cocker Avenue. I made a full recovery. Consequently, in later years I never watched football when I could play it.

My education probably suffered from the illness too. The fact that I was the youngest in my year didn't help either, bearing in mind that I was basically a timid boy. I believe my parents worried about me being sensitive and introverted as a child (Julie was never that way). My dad had wanted to take me to boxing lessons, but mam wouldn't have it. In my teens, mam would occasionally tell me I was too serious; mothers know their children best.

In my early teens, I started to learn to play the piano. I got to the third grade, then stopped. Having been given the 'all clear' from my illness by the doctors, the last thing I wanted was to be indoors sitting at a piano. So my introverted nature diminished as I immediately looked for a football club to join. Fairwater was my first club, but we were not very good. There was little in the way of coaching or fitness training. It was all very amateur, but I loved it! When we played the league leaders, Pontnewydd away, we lost 20-1. I remember because I scored the one – with my head!

At about this time, I joined the Air Training Corp (ATC). In the air cadets I had my first experience of real adventure. We got to co-pilot a Chipmunk single-prop trainer aircraft, as well as gliders. I also found out the hard way what a 'French bed' was. We were spending a week at an RAF base, in Chippenham I think, and were in barracks. At 'lights out' we all climbed into our beds – except I could only get down about two feet into mine. It was dark and deathly quiet so I just stayed there, confused and crunched up in my 'little' bed all night. In the morning I was informed by Gareth Bale, a fellow cadet, that the top sheet of my bed was folded short by a couple of the other lads, for a laugh. I don't think they got much of a laugh as I didn't make a sound all night!

*

"Richard Morgan phoned to let you know he'll be in the sauna suite down the stadium at 3 o'clock tomorrow, if you're interested," mam said. Richard, or Richie as we called him, was a welder, sorry, fabricator; working in Llanwern steel works. He was a family man. It was in his bones. Unless they threw him out of Llanwern, he'd be there for life.

Richie played for the same football club as I did; Cwmbran Catholics (changed to Cwmbran Celtic in later years). I am not a Catholic, but I am not particularly tribal either, so I couldn't see a problem. Fortunately for me, neither could the club. The manager of the under-16 side, Mr Slade, had put me on the left wing where I did my 'wing thing' with relish for years after. Richie also worked continental shifts. Like me, he was probably looking to fill his down day with something enjoyable or interesting. It's Friday tomorrow and I have until 10pm to fill, so I will definitely go.

We had both gone on holiday to Yugoslavia about a year before. I had booked it as a surprise for my girlfriend but she did not want to come, so Richie stepped in at the last moment. The holiday was to Budva in Montenegro. We landed at Dubrovnik airport in Croatia, and were coached south, across the beautiful Dalmatian coastline. We were ferried across deep inlets, matched only by the Norwegian fjords, on the way to the resort.

At this time, Yugoslavia was a socialist republic and included Croatia (where Dubrovnik lay) and Montenegro (which included Budva). Yugoslavia was a short-lived country, established after the first world war as The Kingdom of the Serbs, Croats and Slovenes. The name was changed to Yugoslavia in the late 1920's. After the death of Tito in 1980, ethnic tensions led to a rise in nationalism and war.

We were visiting well before this 'civil war', which erased the Yugoslav state from the map. We saw no animosity at the time and both Croatians and Montenegrins seemed very content in their lovely coastal paradise. The only other country I had visited up to that time was Spain, then under the Franco regime. With Portugal next door still under the influence of Antonio Salazar, Europe had its fair share of authoritarian leaders in the 1960's and 1970's.

We had a great time at Budva, where we relaxed on the beach and took boat trips to inlets for a swim, followed by picnics. It was wonderful, except I couldn't swim! When you cannot swim you take extra care near water. I had tried to learn as a child at Stow Hill public baths in Newport. My dad took me down (although he couldn't swim either). I went under a couple of times and that was it. I had a bit of a phobia after that. On the plane back, Richie pulled out a pair of glass steins, which he had removed from a hostelry as souvenirs! I still have mine to this day, thanks mate.

When we got back from our holiday, I asked Richie to teach me to at least stay afloat. We went to Cwmbran stadium leisure centre and he patiently taught me. Once I could float unaided, I was fine. I learned the basic strokes and felt more relaxed in the water. I am still not a strong swimmer, but I can stay alive if I get wet! My sister learnt in the same place but she was like a water baby compared to me.

*

I think about what to do this morning. It is a strange world when you work continental shifts. There is no daily routine, week in, week out. You are off at strange times, when most other people are working. Then you are working when most people are off. There is also the feeling that the population is cut in half – no one about. I could go back up to my bedroom and read a bit, mostly travel books, adventure and espionage with me. Not today, I would go down to see my friend, Royston Willis, known to us all as Dicker.

The same age as me, Dicker passed his eleven plus exam and went to Abersychan grammar school, north of Pontypool, whereas I failed and went to the local secondary modern school, Coed Eva. My school was modern though, as many schools had to be built to accommodate the large bulge in school children caused by the post war 'baby boom'. I drove down to Dicker's place as I had to keep an eye on the time. He lived just off Star Street, so I turned off Cocker Avenue, south on to Henllys Way, past the park where I spent many hours playing as a child. I turned left at the lower park gate, past the canal.

The canal. As junior school children, we used to come home alongside the canal. One particularly bitter winter, the canal froze over. Instead of walking home alongside, my school friend Nigel Smith and I slid our way along the iced up water. He was close in front when suddenly he disappeared. I just jumped. He'd gone through a hole in the ice, I sailed over it. I remember my instinctive reaction. It must have been instinctive, there was no time to think. Our brains must be working all the time to keep us out of trouble.

By the way, Nigel was OK. I helped him out of the water and we walked to his house. He was soaking wet and freezing, but was more afraid of his mother's wrath when he fronted up. No permanent trauma though. The following summer we were floating down the 'Mississippi' on our made up rafts. Nigel was Huckleberry Finn and I was Davy Crockett.

The canal was also my preferred route home after junior school. At that age, I spent quite a lot of time and energy avoiding being 'picked on'. Being smallish and skinny, I was a target for children 'with problems'. Neil was one such child. He would hound me after school, pushing and shoving me. I always noticed the hostility in such peoples faces; I didn't understand why. That's what upset me the most. It seemed important for him that I should be humiliated.

At home time I would be strategic regarding my route to safety. If I went on the top road, towards the 'top' gate of Cocker Avenue park, I was trapped on Wesley Street if Neil spotted me. By taking the canal route past the school canteen and the 'bottom' gate of the park, I knew I had several escape routes. Once I was over Henllys way and into my estate, I could cut across Fetty Place, Green Acre or Kemys Walk if I was spotted. I did have one advantage; I was quite fast, so I could outrun Neil if I had to. This sort of thing carried over into Secondary school. However, Neil went to Llantarnam whilst I attended Coed Eva.

There are always bullies and victims in schools. By the time I was a fourth year however, I had grown a bit, and filled out, so when Brian (a little smaller than I) tried his luck at humiliating me, I went up to him and grabbed him by the throat, warning him never to try it again. We were fine after that. In fact, I also met Neil in later years and we were also fine. Nature can be cruel. I did, however, come out of my school years with a deep-seated resentment about oppression of all kinds (this has remained with me).

An important diversion from the rough and tumble of secondary school life was the musical concerts organised by the school music teacher, Mrs Brown. An attractive lady (I was beginning to notice!) in her mid to late twenties, I believe. She had the most beautiful touch on the grand piano, which was placed in the main hall. Each morning she would play a piece by Chopin, Beethoven or another of the master composers, as we all marched into assembly. I remember feeling lucky if I sat near enough to see the title on the music sheet she was playing from. I'm afraid I took a while to twig how to pronounce 'Chopin'; not being in a high enough grade to study languages. The music sounded just as good though!

Now, whenever I hear such pieces as Chopin's Nocturne

Op.9 No.2 or Beethoven's beautiful 'Moonlight' sonata No.14 Op 27, I am taken straight back to the delicate charm of her playing. Having attempted to master the instrument myself, I fully appreciated her gift.

But Mrs Brown was much more than just a lovely piano player. She organised concerts, which we would perform for old age pensioners in places such as Oldbury Hall in Old Cwmbran. Pieces from 'The Sound of Music', Gilbert and Sullivan Operetta's and other famous works were performed. All would be skilfully interwoven to create an entertaining evening for the older folks. We enjoyed it very much.

Christmas concerts were always special with Mrs Brown. I well remember playing a pirate in 'The Pirates of Penzance' at one of them, and I have the pics to prove it! There were also parties after the concerts, sometimes at Mrs Brown's home. There was kissing and cuddling to modern music – all harmless fun for adolescents but, sadly, probably not acceptable now.

If you are reading this Mrs Brown – Ann, thank you.

*

Passing the canal, in seconds I was parked outside Dicker's house. He was a really good mate but was also a bit of a rebel. Often unemployed, he was very much in touch with the latest in 'underground music'. Dicker was one of those people who seemed to find things out before everyone else. He was 'in to' bands such as Velvet Underground, Frank Zappa and Iron Butterfly; mostly American leading edge stuff.

As with John in work, I found Dicker fascinating. He never seemed to be down and was always interested in things. This mental energy is a feature of such people. I got tired quite a

31

lot, probably just a side effect of shift work, so mental energy was a precious commodity to me. When I got my two weeks summer holiday or a long weekend off, Dicker and I would often just hit the road in my car. He couldn't drive. We'd been as far as Newcastle in the North East and once, in Carlisle, we cooked our bacon over a single ring gas burner on the floor of my mini, having slept the night in the car. He was taller, but I got the back seat! I definitely had the wander bug.

I also went off camping with friends from both Panteg and school. Again, I drove. It would have to be arranged for the steelworks shutdown; always the last week of July and the first week of August. In Wales, this was known as 'miners fortnight', but was also the compulsory two weeks off which steelworkers had to take.

I well remember one trip when, travelling in a convoy of three cars, the bonnet of the Rover flew up and wrapped itself around the windscreen! Needless to say I pulled over onto the motorway hard shoulder and we got out to take a look. I got some rope from the boot and tied the bonnet down. The bonnet (and boot) on the Rover 2000 is made of aluminium, to keep the weight down, so it bent back down OK. It would keep until after the holiday. This happened on another occasion but this time, I could not get the correct replacement bonnet from the scrap yard. Instead I bought one from a Rover 2000 TC and had that fitted – a significant upgrade!

Something was always running into the Rover. A car pulled out of a junction near Cwmbran stadium one day, and ripped my front offside wing off. Another time, my car was parked outside my parents house and I was asleep off nights. I was told later that a tractor (of all things!) wandered over the road coming up the avenue, and wiped out the front driver's door skin. Again, these are aluminium on a Rover 2000.

"When can we hit the road again Steve?" asked Dicker. "I'm on nights this weekend, so it would be three weeks today, after I finish my last 6-2 shift." "Good," he said. "I have a friend in Liverpool that we could doss with for a couple of nights. A good chance to look around Liverpool, don't you think?" Dicker always did this to me. He had initiative, I am organised. I like to be prepared a bit. The timescale looked reasonable to me, so I said yes. Though I was fascinated by the unknown on our trips, I was always a bit wary of Dicker's 'friends'. They could be a little too socially liberal for me, sometimes. I just observed the choices some people make. I would never take drugs in any form – even smoking is out. I do like a pint, but that's it.

Dicker had one of Frank Zappa's early albums, new to me though. He plays it, I listen. One track, 'Suzy Cream Cheese' for some reason, sticks in my mind. I didn't really understand it, but I did find it interesting, and it passed an hour. Some of the current rock music seemed to reflect anger in a big way. Being lucky with a secure, loving family, I wasn't particularly tuned in to the expression of anger through music. At about noon, I made my way home to dinner.

We call 'lunch' dinner in Wales. How that came about I have no idea. We also call the evening meal 'tea' and not 'dinner'. Funny old world. After a delicious steak and kidney pie made by my mother, I changed for work, packed the sandwiches made by mam and set off.

It's 1:30pm. Back in the Rover, up past the new town and across Station Road. As I drive, I think about my mother or mam as we always called her. She was the centre of our world. She was like a brilliant, but well loved, referee come signalman. She oiled the wheels. The rest of us worked (that is, for money).

Mam made sure we all had what we needed, on time. I'm certain, if organising the world was left to a mother, it would be a vast improvement on the current shambles. If I needed my football kit, ready; sandwiches for work, ready; dinner, tea, supper, etc., all on time and ready. Dad helped too of course and Julie put in. But I was never expected to. Until more recently, I wouldn't have known how! It's a cultural thing, I believe. It was that way when mam was young and it's how she wanted it. In domestic matters, mam always had things the way she wanted.

Unfortunately, although we all liked family holidays, my mother was often not well enough to go. She had an ulcer and had to eat a restricted diet, which resulted in her being rather slim and she got tired sometimes. So the family trips we did manage, to places such as the Scilly Isles, Great Yarmouth and Swanage, hold precious memories.

For me, there was a sense that things were about to change; that my family cocoon was giving way to something else. I didn't think I would choose a family life as an adult. Among my friends, I had seen no evidence that it was the centre of happiness or contentment. My family seemed to be the exception. But what else was out there? Many of my friends were getting married and 'settling down'. Our 'permissive' generation seemed, in the end, to be mostly the same as previous conservative generations. To 'settle down' you must surely first be unsettled. It all felt a bit too comfortable and predictable for me at the time.

Driving past the main gate I came out of my reverie and, after parking up, went to the bathhouse where I got changed for the last 2-10 shift of the week. I pulled my clock card, showing my lucky number 5, and clocked in at 1400 hours.

"Here we go again John!"

Noalimba

Noalimba hostel was barrack room neat,
it was a cul-de-sac off Venus Street.
My memory calls it back quite fondly,
though our journey there was long and lonely.

It was winter time in '81,
that's summer down there, under the sun.
Visas in hand, away from Blighty,
towards the new world, big and mighty.

A sense of adventure held us both,
mixed with anxiety, challenge and personal growth.
Would we measure up out here alone,
or slink back there to a place called 'home'?

The flight, from old to new, it seemed.
Towards the land that I'd long dreamed
of seeing, without expectation,
that I'd ever escape my tired old nation.

My wife and I both felt the same,
it's time to light the adventure flame.
When partners push together one way,
they can often forge a 'go' instead of 'stay'.

Before we could go we needed the points,
from Australia house which permission anoints,
the lucky few who get away.
Then the choice is clear: To go or stay.

West Australia then, it was to be,
Perth, Fremantle and more to see.
No 'assisted passage' for us, so we're free
to go where we want, no government decree.

Just a three month window, the visa read,
only six months married, hardly warmed the bed.
But there's less to pack so we're not slow
to set a date, now it's time to go.

So there we were, just two kids alone,
jet lagged, confused and looking for a phone.
To ring back home to let them know,
we're safely here, we're not too low.

Now reality hits us fair and square,
the awful distance between here and there.
The love we've always felt for kin,
now we feel like leaving was a sin.

We'd lots to do, first jobs to find,
there was little sympathy of any kind.
We found some comfort with other folk
who'd come as we did, we saw the joke.

Our lives came slowly back on track,
Sue got a job, the door opened a crack.
After a while we rented nearby,
still hesitant yet, not ready to fly.

Now we felt we were getting to know,
what we were made of, how we could grow.
Every day, one thing at a time,
we fought to get ourselves over the line.

The emotions you feel when you're out there alone,
with little to no chance of getting back 'home'.
They're special to those who departed their nation,
Noalimba, for us, holds the spirit of migration.

What have we done Sue?

II

We looked around us in shock; the room consisted of painted brick walls within which were squeezed two single beds, placed each side of a small bedside table. There was little room for anything else. Our cases and the box containing my trade tools were at the foot of the beds. There was one window. Above and to the side of 'Sue's' bed, the opening looked out onto a dawning Terra Australis, with beautiful gardens adorned with strange trees and ground plants. There was an agoraphobic vastness to it, which contrasted with our allotted room. There were common ablutions provided on each of the three floors of the block. Everything was clean and fresh but Spartan and un-homely.

Noalimba was built in the 1960's to receive European migrants into Western Australia. The policy of the Commonwealth Federal Government at the time was to encourage young married couples to settle and contribute to the Australian economy – and population! When we arrived, after the Gaugh Whitlam years, Australia's official approach to both indigenous and exogenous peoples was beginning to change. Menzies' 'White Australia' policy was giving way to a new era. The famous handful of dirt held out to Vincent Lingiari in the outback, by Whitlam himself, was a powerful symbol of new rights for the Aboriginal peoples of this vast continent. It was a beginning[3].

So, all in all, we were arriving in a period of optimism and enlightenment. We were just two of the roughly 120,000 migrants (net) who made it to Australia in 1981. This was roughly equal to the 'natural' population expansion of that year, to add to the existing 15 million Australians.

I knew from the start that it was the right place for me. I

grew up loving the idea of living in Australia. My school geography classes were much enlivened when we were allotted one of two world regions to study for our CSE's (Certificate of Secondary Education – inferior to GCE's and preceding GCSE's in the British educational hierarchy of the 1960's).

The two regions were the USA and Australia. America did not stimulate my imagination but Australia certainly did. It seemed to me, even then, to be a bright and happy place. The climate was more to my liking and it was full of space, with lifestyles that we could only dream about in cold damp Britain. Mercifully, I wasn't clever enough to be allocated the USA, so I got Australia. Thus started a process culminating in my standing in this small reception centre room.

I have found that the only people who can fully understand these feelings are fellow migrants. There is also a sense, in the UK, that no one wants to know. It's as though people don't want to see what's outside in case they become unsettled and have to change something. An understandable response I suppose. Anyway, I have always had a soft spot for migrants, from anywhere, ever since.

*

Sue and I were tired from our long journey. A British Airways 747 Jumbo jet (I love those planes) had taken us from our parents and family back home and, via Kuala Lumpur (fuel stop), deposited us in Perth Western Australia. It had been my choice. I had got it down to two places – Brisbane and Perth. My cousin, Gareth, had been to both places (and a lot more) during his time in the merchant navy. He thought both were lovely, but Perth was set next to the wonderful Indian Ocean and had many miles of beaches stretching north and south. There was little heavy industry.

Kwinana steel works, south of Perth, was looking like it could fold, leaving only mining and power stations. However, there was much in the way of medium to light industry.

I decided that I would sacrifice my industrial knowledge – if necessary – to gain a foothold in this place. Sue supported my decision. She was a clerk typist. Her work could be done anywhere, so long as it was in English! So Perth it was. We felt it was very important to be honest with each other about what we wanted to get out of this decision. We both felt that adventure was key, though many others prioritised economic advancement. As it turned out, Perth, with its booming housing market and growing population, was a good choice for both.

It wasn't as simple as that of course. After we married in July 1980, we applied to Australia House, in London, for permission to emigrate. As most people know, Australia operates a points system; it was in use back then. The most points went to relatives of Australians, but we had none. Next in line came skills. We both had some of those. They had to be in demand and be recognised as equivalent to those in Australia. For example, my four-year electrical apprenticeship in Panteg steelworks had to be at least equivalent to its Australian opposite number. It was! An important hurdle was overcome, as my work carried more points and was in greater demand than Sue's. So, between us we had just enough points to pass the first hurdle.

Next we were invited for an interview in The Strand, the location of Australia House in London. We went by train. Arriving in 'the big smoke', Sue and I were walking nervously towards this appointment with our future when she went over awkwardly on her high-heeled shoe. The heel had broken off. Sue wanted to call it off. She was very upset, not wanting to be interviewed with one leg shorter than the other!

This was one of those key moments for us. I was desperate inside, but I kept my head and coolly explained that this was our one and only chance to get a ticket out. "Now or never," I said, holding my breath for the answer. Thankfully, Sue agreed to carry on. We were told that we were not eligible for the assisted passage programme (unlike Owen), but that we had been accepted for the self-funding visa, pending routine medical check-ups. I was over the moon.

Because I was an electrician and therefore needed to accurately determine wire colours etc., I was required to undergo eye tests for colour blindness. We both had to be checked for TB, which was about in the UK at the time. We went back to London for these tests. When we were cleared they told us we would receive our visas to enter Australia sometime in the winter (1980/81). These were known as 'permanent settlement' visas. Once we had received them, we would have three months to use them before they expired.

There was a lot going on in the UK around this time. In particular, the political situation was deteriorating, as the struggle between the conservative government and the industrial working classes moved into the orbit of steel making. Known to history as the 'winter of discontent', the steelworkers were getting militant. Ostensibly it was for higher wages, but there was strong sympathy for our 'brothers' in the mines who had been in the front line of this defensive battle of ideologies[4].

I felt deep down that there could only be one winner, and it wouldn't be us. I was in the union. Most 'blue collar' workers were in those days. We were a 'closed shop'; that is to say, if you wanted to work at Panteg, you had to join one of the unions. I was fine with that. I knew by instinct that working class people (no one admits to being that now) only held *collective* strength against other institutions and power groups. Incongruously, U2 were pushing into the musical future with their album 'Boy' while, in the freezing January of 1981, I took my turn at the brazier defending the past.

A month later the letter arrived from Australia House. Our visas were in it. My visions of leaving my exhausted and darkened country for the optimism and brightness of lovely Perth were stronger than ever. We had just to find the strength to say goodbye to our loved ones. At about this time, my sister Julie and her husband Mark had their car give up the ghost. I promised the Rover to them.

*

Emigrating to Australia in those days felt like going to the moon. You didn't expect to see your loved ones again for a long time, if ever. The end of loving relationships is always hard, but both Sue and I had experienced it before. We had both been engaged previous to our meeting. Sue was betrothed to a drummer in a Welsh band; a pursuit which took him all over the place. It ended badly when he was drawn to another girl with a similar musical obsession.

For me the relationship had lasted about five years, off and on, from aged sixteen to twenty-one. However, being a dreamer, the idea of adventure and travel was quietly growing inside me. This was complimented by a sense that I didn't want my life to work out the way my parents' lives had. Bearing in mind that the cultural mood music of the day was still liberal and experimental, I didn't want to settle down in a council house before I knew what life was all about. But there was something else; all too frequently my friends' families seemed to be unhappy adversarial affairs, with a man and woman trapped together waging war on each other. That was my nightmare scenario.

I've always been a late developer, young in my school year (born August 25th) so, while my mates seemed to be happy to settle into domestic bliss, I resisted. It was not helped by what I felt was a lack of trust between us, which caused me to hold back. We did eventually get engaged, but I think my betrothed sensed my reluctance to go further.

Things came to a head during one crazy moment in a country pub when she took off her ring and placed it on the table in front of me. Bewildered, I felt obliged to pocket it. She had forcefully accused me of looking at another girl. I was shocked! I had not done this, and told her so repeatedly. My protests were shut down. It was made clear to me that I had looked, when in fact I hadn't. I have many faults but I was indignant that she thought I could behave that way. Also, I do not have a 'casual relationship' with the truth.

I didn't know how to defend myself, but I knew my sense of integrity would never allow me to accept that I had done wrong. Was this the beginning of the 'nightmare scenario'? Strangely, we never discussed it again. It's amazing what jealousy and poor communication can do!

There was also the feeling that I was just an institutional accessory; that it was all about the ring. I think engagement rings can promote divisiveness. Firstly, they imply 'ownership' of the girl as well as 'dependency' by the boy; secondly, the ring can be used as a weapon in a heated argument. No ring, no weapon to hurt with.

It became clear that we were pulling in different directions. Eventually, my girlfriend moved in with a mutual friend and that was that. The relationship had run its course. I am grateful that I do not possess a ruthless streak. I'd taken no action to hurt anyone and I had not cheated or betrayed; having arguably been honest to the point of naivety. We were like two objects colliding in space, both heading off into new and different orbits. I wondered where my new orbit would take me.

On the plus side, I felt the boy in me was finally giving way to the man. Also, in subsequent relationships I found that the 'green eyed monster' no longer affected me. I had long realised that jealousy was a destructive emotion that needed to be suppressed, so I was glad to be rid of it.

Being young and strong, I was determined to move forward towards something more positive. I was aged twenty-one by this time and Mike Oldfield's 'Tubular Bells' was my music of choice. Growing within me was an appreciation that I could now shape my life as I wished. The scent of a more adventurous and less predictable future was beginning to pass under my nose.

*

An opportunity to go for a weekend of parachute jumping in Herefordshire came – out of the blue! The invitation came from my friend Michael (Monty) Wright. He was a former soldier in the Guards, having been to Belize and elsewhere with his regiment. He was now a policeman and had settled into married life with Julie, a school friend of my sister Julie.

The event was to be held at Shobdon airfield, a small village in the beautiful north of rural Herefordshire. Shobdon has an impressive history, being the place that glider crews were trained for the Normandy landings of 1944. Since 1962 it has been a civilian airfield.

On the way up I asked Monty what we were letting ourselves in for. "It's static line," he said. Wonderful, I thought. "What's that?" I asked. "You don't have to pull your own chute open, though you go through the drill as though you had to." I remembered seeing second world war films where parachute regiment soldiers would jump out of a plane one by one, each attached or 'hooked on' by a ribbon cord. At the full extent of this cord, the parachute would open and the soldier would just have to guide himself to the desired landing spot. Simple then!

We were to have a training session on the Saturday morning, followed by our first jump in the afternoon. On Sunday we were to jump again, after a recap (good idea, I thought). The training session was thorough, as you would expect if you intend to step into mid air with just a piece of material to slow you down. We were taken to a hanger and shown the different types of parachute and then witnessed the packing of our own chutes for the first jump. This was done by the experts – reassuring. They also packed the emergency chute; the one that you have to open manually if your main chute fails to open. Monty and I paid close attention.

Next we went outside and, after climbing a small scaffold, were shown how to 'bend and roll' on landing. The landing would take place at a deceptive speed so technique was essential to avoid injury. Like I said, they were thorough.

Finally our turns came for the actual first jump. The aeroplane that was to take us up was a Cessna single engine four-seater; quite cramped but never mind, we would be leaving it shortly! Monty and I went together. It was made clear to us that, should we 'chicken out', we would be pushed out for the safety of the plane. So, once we were off the ground, the only way down was by parachute.

"One thousand and one, one thousand and two…" I shouted as I fell through the air, up to one thousand and five, then I put my hand across my chest and pretended to pull my rip-cord, after which the chute deployed and I called "parachute open correctly" (after looking up to check, of course).

After the noise of the Cessna and the adrenalin rush of the build up and jump, the next three minutes were the most relaxing of my life to date. The 360-degree view was simply stunning as I sat in my harness and looked about myself. I had jumped first and now had to steer myself, with the use of a toggle in each hand, towards the spot reserved for us to land. I did OK, avoiding injury. The sense of achievement was an important feeling for me. I had taken on my fear and overcome it. I felt I had grown. The evening meals and drinks tasted especially good that Saturday as Monty and I basked in our new found bravery. However, we had to do it all again tomorrow.

Sunday morning and, after the recap we were taken to the hanger... to pack our own parachutes! We did this ever so carefully and then out we went for jump number two. If doing it once was a challenge, the second time was worse. I have learned this about life in general. Difficult things always seem harder the second time – at least for me. However, it went very well again, and we were awarded our certificates to prove we had been trained to the level required to jump from a plane. I have never done it since, but I have never regretted doing it. The years of rheumatic fever, when I was feeble and ill, were well and truly in the past.

I found out much later that my father's older brother, Arthur, was in one of the parachute regiments during the Normandy landing. He was one of those dropped behind the German lines. Respect.

*

By the time I met Sue I was 24 years old, with one eye on my settled life of football and work, and the other on breaking out. The heat wave summer of 1976 had come and gone, along with Al Stewart's superb album 'Year of the Cat'. I still had no firm idea about the shape my future might take. I just felt that life could offer much more if I didn't just sit back passively.

I was still living with my parents and enjoying a normal social life. One evening, I was sitting in the bar of my local with a friend from work, Mike Street, when he asked if I was going to Fred Jagger's retirement do. Fred was a senior day shift electrician in Panteg; an ex union rep of many years, who basically helped us apprentices get jobs as electricians with the steelworks when our 'indentures' were completed. We felt very warmly towards Fred, so we decided to go.

The Conifers hotel was situated just down the road from Cwmbran football and athletics stadium, about two miles from Cocker Avenue, where I lived. Mike and I went in and, after the speeches for Fred, we relaxed into a drink and some dancing. I got up to dance with a girl called Jane. She indicated that her sister, who was working behind the bar, recognised me from our time at the local college in Pontypool. Sue had lovely long dark hair and eyes that looked right into your soul. I asked her out.

Sue lived in Sebastopol, an estate south of Pontypool near to where I worked. I remember when I arrived at her house for our first date, her father said he could hear my Rover coming up the hill. He always called my car 'thumper' after that. Mr Taylor had worked in heavy industry all his life, except when he was conscripted for 'national service', as young men were in his day. He was currently working in Llanwern Steelworks Newport, also a BSC concern, but much larger. He had, however, spent some years working in the now defunct 'merchant mill' at Panteg. We were therefore able to talk 'steelworker' language to each other; not swearing mind you, just banter we were both comfortable with.

I knew straight away that Sue was different. There was a spark. I found out that, although she was three and a half years younger, Sue was in just about the same place in life that I was. As I came to know her better, I realised that Sue never used jealousy as a weapon. There was an intrinsic loyalty about her, which appealed to me greatly. I felt that I could trust this lovely person with my heart – so I did!

Sue was also restless and looking to break out, but was thinking of Canada. We were sitting in the lounge of the Tavern pub in Hollybush one evening, just down the road from Cocker Avenue. She was wearing a lovely top with a maxi skirt. I felt very proud. I moved her quickly on from Canada to Australia. We did consider South Africa; I had a work mate, Paul, who had emigrated there, but he then returned to settle down. We felt we could not accept the apartheid system, which existed in South Africa at the time, so we rejected it. We decided to investigate Australia further. Now, while I am a dreamer, Sue is a doer, so by the time we married in July 1980 we were ready to apply for emigration. The process was under way!

I remember how hard it was to pack my job in. Panteg had been a brutal but benevolent environment in which to learn about work and, indeed, life in general. However, it is safe to say that it was a rather narrow world view – something I was setting out to broaden. As a blue collar worker I was required to give two weeks notice. A few of my mates came to a local pub for a fair-well drink and that was it. After twelve years I was on the outside. Of course, I didn't know it at the time, but I would never work in a steelworks again.

*

The minibus was full. Aboard were my parents, Sue's parents and Grandmother; my sister Julie with Mark, as well as Sue's sister Jane and her husband to be, Mike. Add in my toolbox and our luggage, with Sue and I, and we were full. A few miles down the road we noticed that my Dad remained sitting on the step by the central door. Sue's mum invited him to sit next to her, but he said he was fine where he was. My dad was unusual sometimes! Julie was pregnant at the time. It was the 29th of March. Jemma was subsequently born on the 1st of August 1981 (the first of three for Julie). Since her birthday read as 1.8.81 I had no trouble remembering it!

Of course we were all quite stressed out and I have to admit I would never again say such a goodbye at an airport. At Heathrow check-in I had trouble getting my toolbox through. It was too heavy. I pleaded to the girl at the desk that I was emigrating and needed my tools to work. She took a second look at my passport, noticing that my surname was Woods; hers was too. She waved us through, we were on our way. We boarded and took our seats in economy class. Sue was by the window, I was in the middle and a lady from Boyup Brook, half a day south of Perth, was outside me. We were emotional and I noticed that the Australian to my right was also emotional. Within the hour, both Sue and the Australian were crying. I held it together in the centre. The 'Australian' was in fact an ex-pat Brit who had emigrated years before. She was back to see her mum, who had sadly died before her daughter could get there. What a start to our adventure.

The journey was a long one, sleeping and reading the time away. We disembarked for the plane to refuel in Kuala Lumpur, before the final leg south to Perth. It was late at night before we stepped out onto Australia for the first time. Despite my fatigue, I filed the special moment away in my memory. After customs and baggage recovery we got a taxi to take us to Noalimba, in a suburb called Bateman, south of the Swan river. It seemed very dark as we were driven through the suburbs. The houses were far back from the road, with trees in front of the windows. We thought this strange until later, when we felt the heat from the Australian sun!

After what seemed like an age, the Ford Falcon Swan taxi (they were always white – I quickly came to understand why) dropped us at our destination where a night watchman led us to our block. Up an open concrete staircase and into our 'home' for the next eight weeks. The local time was about 4am. We collapsed exhausted onto our beds, too tired to care about anything.

The watchman had informed us that we were required to attend our reception meeting at 9am; no ifs or buts. We were groggy but up at 8am. After much needed showers in our respective ablution blocks, we headed for reception. On the way, a Welsh couple passed us and said, "It's OK here as long as you can get a job." We grabbed a snack at the canteen and then presented ourselves for inspection by Phil, the personnel officer. This was our first encounter with an Australian wearing what I can best describe as a boy scouts outfit. Shorts and knee length socks, all khaki, with town shoes on. It was normal gear for many dinky-di's, we later discovered.

Phil firmly advised us to forget our families as they would forget us, in time. We knew this was not true but nevertheless it upset us even more than we were already. I was beginning to suspect that the ideology was based on a military model.

After reading us some basic 'camp' rules, Phil told us to jump in his (government provided) Sigma station wagon. Off we went down Leach highway, heading west towards Fremantle. I remember this journey well as the car radio was belting out 'Betty Davis Eyes' via 96fm, a local radio station. On arrival, we were led to an office block where we signed on; we were now in the Australian tax and benefits system. I had wandered a long way. As a child, I followed my older friend Lyn Goman to his school, unbeknown to my mother! Going walkabout at just four years old.

A Letter from Sydney [circa 1983]

Arrived here on the red eye, cracking dawn.
Out of Kingsford Smith and up Parramatta road,
we're staying, so I'm told.
Just seven days working here, I hope
to see some sights around the bay.
I'm loving it already, this short stay.

I'll fix the Hills Hoist when I return,
but right now I've got rubber to burn.
We've worked all day, now I'm on my way
to see the Opera House, today's the day.
Then I hope to get a ferry, out to Manly
if there's time, or else I'll do it Tuesday.

The Sydney folk are very friendly,
there's a relaxed feel that Perth should envy.
The four of us are staying in digs, rent free.
The firm will pay the bill from its money tree.
They'll be ahead, our pound of flesh
takes at least ten hours a day to fetch.

I'm missing you, so far away,
it's over three thousand k's.
You and I, more isolated now,
from our folk and each other. Round the bay,
everyone is gearing up for the Americas cup.
It's tomorrow night, I think I'll stay up.

Allan Bond won it with Australia two,
I watched it on TV, all night through.
He's from WA [he's really expat Brit],
but I feel proud, I must admit.
The job is dragging, but I'm glad,
to turn down this trip I'd have been mad.

It's nice to know your job was a good sell,
in the city, TUTA, the union people, as well.
If you're lucky you'll get that trip
to Melbourne and Sydney, let it rip!

I hope all's well with the old Falcon,
she's ageing now, but who needs air-con.

Unfortunately I didn't get across
the Coat Hanger, there just wasn't time.
We did OK according to my boss,
the job was done, it all went fine.
I'm tiring now, though it was fun
to race around this town, under the sun.

I'm booked to fly Ansett, Friday, midnight run,
I'll be back in Perth not later than 3am.
I know you'll be there at the airport,
I'll see you then, hope you like what I bought.
It's Thursday so I'll post this letter pronto
and hope you get it, love you also.

Settling in

III

Where to begin? There was a lot to do. When you normally build your life, it tends to happen incrementally, in a sort of naturally evolving way. Not so with migration. You have to set it all up quickly, so we had to get organised (Sue is strong in this department). We would have to learn fast.

We soon found out that, straight after breakfast in the canteen, the phone booths outside the main office at Noalimba were chock-a-block with migrants calling prospective employers, seeking that elusive first job. People were walking back and forth purposefully with copies of 'The West Australian' folded to the jobs pages under their arms. Sue and I realised that we couldn't take the next step without one of us scoring a job.

We had been to Applecross to open our account with The Commonwealth Bank, noticing that our lowly seven thousand pounds Stirling would get us just ten thousand Dollars Australian. We blew two thousand dollars on a Toyota van. I thought it would be useful moving things about in the near future. I'm not much good with cars and I admit to making a mistake with this one! Still, we were mobile.

Sue struck first. The Teachers college at Claremont, over on the west side of Perth, took her on as a clerk typist. This allowed us to start looking for a rental. It came just in time as we had used up our allotted six weeks in Noalimba. We were, however, permitted to stay a further two weeks, then – out. We were well into the first extra week. We started looking around the neighbouring suburbs for suitable accommodation.

We loved Applecross and Bullcreek, but both were too expensive. We disliked the weatherboard houses in the older suburbs surrounding Fremantle and we were reluctant to go up to the northern suburbs, as many migrants did. Finally we found a place in Allerton Way, Booragoon. It was a three-bed bungalow type duplex (almost all houses seemed to be bungalow type in Perth at this time). It was also near the Swan river and just over Leach Highway from Bateman.

It was here that Sue saw her first Goanna. These are lizard type creatures, indigenous to Australia. They vary in length. This one, she said, came out of the scrub opposite us, crossed the road and waddled up our drive. It then stopped and basked in the sun. Sue went next door to ask the neighbour what it was. Learning that it was harmless, she just sat and watched this amazing and exotic (to us) creature, until it slowly turned around and retreated over the road and back into the bush.

At about this time, Sue and I went to see if we could find where my Panteg workmate John McGrath's brother was buried. We knew he had lived in an older Fremantle suburb, so we started there. We literally knocked doors, asking if anyone remembered the incident and which cemetery would have been used. One older couple did recall the tragedy, but could remember little more. They did however tell us that Patrick would have been buried in Karrakatta cemetery.

Sue and I bought flowers and went to Karrakatta to find where Patrick lay. There was a listing in the office and, locating the grave, we cleaned it up a little. Placing the flowers down, I felt we were doing a very important and even sacred thing for John's mum. Something she would have never been able to do. We later sent a letter to John for his mum. We hoped it brought some comfort.

I was having problems finding work as an industrial

electrician. This was because I needed a state electrical licence to work unsupervised. I had gone to the State Energy Commission in Wellington Street Perth to apply for my licence. They informed me that all my qualifications were in order, and that I could sit the next set of theory and practical exams at Mount Lawley College. Fortunately, I was never informed of this examination process at the migration interview in London, or I may never have emigrated. Still, I accepted this and enquired when it could take place. "You've just missed the exams for this year so you will have to sit them early next year," I was told. It was not June yet. "How can I find work?" I asked. I was told I could work anywhere that one electrical licence holder was already working.

Now, unlike industrial Britain, many of Perth's medium and light industries were just one spark big, so finding a two spark factory was difficult. Nevertheless, I took up the challenge, refusing to be defeated at this early stage of my new life. I did however write to the Liberal party deputy Premier of WA, Ray O'Connor, pointing out the unnecessary stress that this system was placing on migrants. O'Connor went on to replaced Sir Charles Court (Lib) as Premier in 1982, and was himself replaced by Brian Burke (ALP) in 1983.

Premier O'Connor, and his replacement Burke, were later jailed for the improper involvement of the WA government with big business (WA Inc.). A reassuring sign that no one here was above the law. Burke did, however, abolish capital punishment in WA during 1984.

*

While I was applying for jobs, I decided to take lessons as a Semi-Trailer (articulated lorry) driver. I fancied the life of a driver. Travelling through the outback etc. appealed to my adventurous streak. After about half a dozen lessons I sat and passed both theory and practical tests. However I recall a particularly ropey manoeuvre where I was required to back the trailer around a corner. The examiner looked at me and asked if I had a driving job to go to. When I answered no, he said I had passed!

I never got to use my semi-trailer licence. I answered an advert for an electrician at a steel reinforcing manufacturer (the stuff that goes into cement based buildings). ARC Engineering was located in the industrial area in, of all places, Welshpool. I was interviewed by a young English plant engineer called Alan Carr. There was an incumbent electrician in place, a really nice older Australian by the name of Jim Morris. The engineer liked me and offered me the job, as long as I would undertake mechanical duties as well. Clearly this young Englishman was on the make, and saw the opportunity to exploit me. Normally, I would feel my temperature rise at any sign of oppression; of me or anyone else. But I was in my dream country and it didn't seem to matter as much.

Thus began my work as a combined skills workshop tradesman. ARC was in the opposite direction to where Sue worked in Claremont, so each workday morning, we would head east on Leach to take me to ARC, before she went west to Claremont. Then she'd come back for me at the end of the day. A long day, but we now had two pay packets coming in. We decided to manage with just the Toyota for the time being.

Buying a second car would have to wait, as we decided to buy some land and 'build a house' on it. This is what most migrants did in Perth at the time. 'Double brick and tile' we were told when we attended a seminar in Newport, South Wales, before we came. So we did. We chose the suburb of Thornley. It was on the road to Gosnells, heading inland. We secured a 'block' (land comes in blocks, not plots, in Australia) in Grundy way. It was on a corner, something we thought might be an advantage but, in fact, most Aussies avoided, as it meant more watering of useless land. Water is expensive in a dry country. You live and learn.

It is worth mentioning here that Perth, unlike the other major cities in Australia, is built on sand. Yes sand; it is a slightly darker colour than beach sand. This being so, house building methods then and now include laying a 'slab' of concrete on a levelled patch of prepared builders sand. Once the slab is set, the brickies can start to lay internal and external walls on it. I believe this is the way that weight is evenly distributed on the sand below. It must also be quicker and cheaper than the more traditional foundation method. Note, large structures such as city apartments, skyscrapers etc. did not, of course, use this method.

One advantage with Thornley was that it had a tennis club. I tweaked my knee a couple of years before we emigrated and had to give up football. Unwisely, I had turned up to play for my then football club, Cwmbran Celtic, after working the night shift. The pitch was rock hard with deep divots. I caught my left boot in one as I came down from heading a ball, and dislocated my left knee (very painful). Later, I got a semi-retired professional sports physio to put it back in; there was cruciate ligament damage. However, it was fine for everyday use, as long as I kept the muscles holding it together toned up, which I did.

I had always loved tennis and I became a member of Thornley tennis club; causing problems with my lefty serve and topspin forehand, not much else mind! Though, I did manage to beat the club champion, Steven White in my first match; he never let that happen again. Predictably, my favourite tennis player was Rod Laver, the Australian left hander. He is the only player to win two Grand Slams (not just Grand Slam titles); winning all four majors in the same calendar year (Australian, French, British and American), twice.

Having selected the house to put on the block (a modest three bed bungalow called the 'Banksia' by the developer), we commissioned it. There were many design and build companies in Perth at the time and we went with a rep whose sir name was Taylor, Sue's maiden name. To be fair, Plunkett (the company name) were very good and Rosemary (the rep's first name) helped us choose everything from the kitchen worktops to the number and location of socket outlets in each room. (At the time of writing, we have still not achieved this level of customer service in the UK.)

Meanwhile, we were enjoying our young lives by going to hotels to see local bands and dance. We went to the Booragoon hotel many times, often to see 'The Helicopters'. You went to hotels in Australia, for pub-come-nightclub life. We also went to 'The Old Melbourne' in the Central Business District (CBD) to see the bigger Australian bands such as Men at Work, Icehouse and later, Real Life. We even saw INXS in their early years in a northern suburbs hotel.

During this time I became familiar with the local brew. The Perth beer market was dominated by the Swan brewery, in Canning Vale, acquired by the British ex-pat businessman Alan Bond[5]. You could get two types of lager beer, both had to be freezing cold to drink. The normal beer was just called 'Swan'. The stronger stuff was called 'Emu'; it kicked like one too! You bought it in 'stubbies', which were about a half pint. At a bar, you would have it from the tap in a 'middy'; a small glass which came straight from the fridge to keep the beer cold. The parlance was 'standard' or 'super', after the two types of petrol available at the time.

By the way, you never put your own fuel in the car at a petrol station, an attendant always did that. Similarly, you never packed your own bags at the supermarket. We felt spoilt!

I learned to stay on Swan after we went into Fremantle to have an evening of entertainment and to explore. We went into a bar and started to play pool with some young Aboriginal boys. I'm not too bad at pool, but we were hustled good and proper. Fair play to them, they knew greenhorns when they saw them. From here, the evening was about to get even better. We went out onto the street and, mindful that it was nearing 'shut tap', went into a bar a few doors down. We ordered our ice cold middies and sat down. Sue noticed a big guy going to the door, which he closed, locking it after. He then returned to his seat. We got a bit anxious about this until we realised that it was a 'lock-in'. Listening to the banter, we found out that they were all off-duty members of the WA police. I can't remember how we got home that night, but we had a great time.

While we were still living in Booragoon, there was a knock on the door one day and I answered it to none other than Owen, my friend from Panteg. It was great to see him. I said "it's a small world" and he agreed. He'd left New South Wales with his wife Deb, and headed for Perth and a job with Solar Edwards. This was one of the two big solar water heating companies about at the time. Owen said they were renting in the Midland/Guildford area, north east of Perth. We met up several times after that. I felt Owen was integrating really well into the Australian lifestyle.

*

Not long after, we moved into our brand new home. It was just a shell really, needing plenty of work both inside and out. But, having secured a loan from the 'Home Building

58

Society', we were mortgagees for the first time! Before we left, Sue rearranged the letterbox in Booragoon by reversing into it with the Toyota. I should add that most letterboxes were brick affairs mounted to the side of the drive. We also took custody of our first pet. We brought him back from ARC one evening. He was one of a litter of kittens from the works cat. I remember us putting him in a box for the night in a spare bedroom, but he got out and, with much commotion, climbed up the sheets into our bed. He stayed there all night. We didn't have the heart to put him back in his box. We then found he liked to climb the net curtains at the windows, so we decided to call him Dennis, after the menace; a character in the British comic magazine for children called 'The Beano'.

Encouragement to get the work done on our new house, as well as get a second car, came when we heard from Sue's parents that they wanted to come over for a holiday to see us. After looking about for a better deal than we got with the Toyota, we finally ignored the dealers (a crooked lot in Perth at the time), and bought a Ford Falcon privately. The Falcon was old, but she was solid – and heavy. She was a six cylinder station wagon with bench seats and column change automatic transmission. There was also a big rust hole in the passenger side floor! Looking just like one of the old American automobiles, we loved her. She cost us 500 Australian Dollars (we sold her four years later, for the same amount). We went to drive-in cinemas around Perth, reversing her up so we could drop the tailgate (it was hot of course) and watch the film from the spacious fold down rear seat. I remember we saw the Australian war drama Gallipoli that way, at nearby Willetton.

We got the Falcon just in time, as the Toyota was starting to play up. The problem in Perth is that the local water is bad for car engines. Also, being close to the ocean, there was a high level of salt in the air. The Toyota eventually gave up and we got it towed away. We were back to one car. Somehow, it just didn't matter. We were living in the moment.

One day we went to a house party in Roleystone, up in the hills. We had a great time, probably too great a time, as we were both drunk and we still had to drive home. For the hour and a half it took us to get home we shared the driving; no, I mean actually shared it! I was behind the wheel but Sue could see a bit better, so she steered while I did everything else. Almost home, we waved our way down Yale road, just needing to take a turn into Grundy way less than 100 metres away, when we swerved and just missed flying into the paddock to the right. We were very lucky that night, no question; but we were young. I know, that is becoming my stock excuse.

It was now April 1982. We had been in Australia for over a year. I had sat and passed my electrical tests a month before, and was issued with my class A licence as an 'electrical fitter/mechanic'; so that was sorted. I had also completed a 'digital techniques' course at Mount Lawley Tech', to fill some gaps in my knowledge. Sue had got a job in the city (the CBD) with TUTA (The Trade Union Training Authority).

This organisation was a world first, operating between 1975 and 1996[6]. TUTA was a Commonwealth Government sponsored entity, set up to facilitate smooth relations between the unionised workforce and employers, as well as promoting industrial democracy. Arguably this was an enlightened attempt at consensual relations, contrasting sharply with both the anti-union stance of previous State Premier Sir Charles Court, and the situation in Britain.

One day, a Telecoms engineer called at TUTA to carry out some work on the phone system. His name was Richard and he immediately picked up Sue's accent (to my ears, Sue was taking on a distinctly Australian lilt, a result of communication being key to her work). Richard, who it turns out was from Cardiff, knew that it was of Welsh origins. He is a gregarious person and soon introduced himself, explaining that he and his wife Marion had passed through Noalimba, a month or so before us. "Small world again" was what Sue thought. Richard then invited us both to Belmont Park on Saturday evening, to see the trots. This is a form of Australian harness racing where the jockey sits on a small two-wheeled gig, with reigns controlling the horse in front. The horse is prevented from galloping by 'hopples' placed around its legs[7]. Sue said yes, and we looked forward to an interesting evening in the city.

Belmont Park is in the East Perth area, near the famous WACA cricket ground. We met Richard and Marion outside, and they introduced us to Ralf and Dawn, also ex-Noalimba and from the Swansea area of Wales. The evening was clearly going to be an all Welsh affair! It was a very interesting outing. As well as making new (lifelong) friends, we discovered some of the mysteries of the trots – known more correctly as 'pacing'.

Neither Sue nor I had ever been into a betting shop, never mind onto a course. We were soon surrounded by the noisy confusion of the excited 'punters' rushing to the TAB windows to place bets such as 'trifecta's' and 'quinella's'. We had a go; advised how to do so by our new Welsh friends. Of course, we won nothing. But I don't think that's the point for most people who go to such occasions. It seemed to me to be some excitement and fun after a week of work; and Australians certainly know how to have fun! They work to live and not the other way around. I found this all very refreshing compared to the repressed nature of life in the UK.

My father used to go once a week to Derek Pugh's betting shop in Old Cwmbran, to put a bet on the gee-gees. It was one of his very few pleasures, and he was very careful not to over-do it. My dad was a quiet family man, happy to give almost all he earned up to mam, to be used for housekeeping and for things his children needed. He was one of the many decent silent heroes of the age. My mother was happy for him to bet on horses, as long as he didn't pull me into it. She needn't have worried, as I found the whole betting environment to be an element of British working class culture that I found seedy and shabby.

Our Welsh friends had moved up to the northern suburbs after their respective stays at Noalimba. Whereas Booragoon offered good access to the Beautiful Swan river as well as the city, the north was a narrow corridor of suburbs so that the lovely Perth beaches to the west were more accessible. We went up to see our new friends when we could, and we would all go off to have a barbecue on the beach – quite often for free. The barbie electricity was often laid on by the ocean side communities for the benefit of all. A different world indeed.

I remember Ralf and Dawn had a Holden Kingswood. This is an iconic car in Australia, being the home made brand, as it were. As with almost all cars in WA at the time, the Kingswood had six, or perhaps eight cylinder engines. I often saw Ralf with his head under the bonnet trying to solve some problem or other with it. We were also working as fast as we could to prepare our house at this time, as Sue's parents were due later in the month.

*

It was great to see Sue's mum and dad. They had come via Hong Kong. Sue's dad had spent much of his conscription years as a gunner in the Royal Artillery there, so it brought back memories for him. They spent one night in Hong Kong, but it was the rainy season and it did just that – in buckets. They almost missed their connection to Perth as the taxi failed to turn up. They got to the airport in a wet rush, but Sue's mum was very anxious for a while. Sue's dad made use of the free drinks aboard the 747, so he got over it pretty quickly!

It was still the hot season in Perth. We had no air conditioning but were pretty acclimatised by this time. Sue's parents had the larger spare room but, coming out of a British winter, they were sweltering in the heat. As soon as the sun went down all the windows and doors would be flung open to allow the heat to escape. This was OK because the flies (WA has a lot of flies) were kept out by the fly screens over all openings. We had explained that the afternoons were a little cooler owing to the 'Fremantle doctor' – a breeze, which regularly wafted across the city to cool its overheated inhabitants. Sue's mum felt the heat most and, in desperation, would ask when the 'afternoon doctor' was coming.

They had just six weeks with us, so we made the best use of the time. Sue and I had to work some of that time, but when we were off we did lots. We found out that two local wineries were running boat trips up the Swan river to their respective vineyards, so that customers could sample their wares. On the way upriver there were meals aboard which all could enjoy whilst admiring the view. It sounded great. The vineyards were Haughtons and Sandelfords. We chose Haughtons and booked it. On the day, we all had a lovely tipsy time of it and saw some of Perth's beautiful suburbs from a different perspective. I found that West Australian businesses were not mean or begrudging in their treatment of customers. In fact, the culture of the place as a whole was one in which everyone seemed to know they were very lucky to be there.

We also took them to Willetton drive-in cinema where we all watched ET. They thought this was just like they imagined American drive-ins to be. We agreed. One day, Sue's dad came to work with me so he could meet everyone (he's always been gregarious). On another occasion, we went with our Welsh friends in convoy up to Yanchep national park, north of Perth. On the way, the Falcon had a flat tyre and Mr 'T' hurt his back helping me change the wheel. He never mentioned it though; didn't want to spoil the fun!

It was one of those days with the Falcon and, on the way up a steep gradient, it started to overheat. Now we always knew that some of the engine cylinders didn't work properly, but we had six so we felt we had some 'redundancy'. We'd been told to put an egg in the radiator if it boiled over. So we did – and it worked! I put one in every so often after that, just in case.

We took an excursion to Margaret River, which was a small settlement in the south west of the state at the time. Sue and her mum sat in a coffee shop overlooking the river while her dad and I hired a canoe to paddle up the river – wonderful fun, and we didn't fall in.

On another occasion, Mr Taylor and I went to the WACA to see Australia play Pakistan, I think. It started to rain before the start of the match, so we wondered if we would see any cricket that day. It stopped and the sun came out, but the pitch was still too wet, so the WACA called the channel 9 helicopter in to dry it. That's right, it hovered over the pitch so it's rotor blades could dry off the damp surface! We got to see the game. Australia won, of course.

Inevitably, the day came when Sue's parents returned to Blighty. We were very sad, but took consolation in the fact that we had given them the holiday of a lifetime. At about this time, Sue and I had decided to expand the family – so we went to a kennel and chose a pedigree Rough Collie. We named him Kel, and he would travel more in his life than most humans. Being a pedigree, we had agreed to show him in dog shows around Perth. Sue took an enthusiastic role in this, with much loving care for our new family member. Dennis didn't blink an eye. As long as he was fed and watered, he was fine. Bonneyboy Brigadier was Kel's pedigree name, so that's what went on any rosettes he won. He did win a few, but we learned which judges preferred the English or American types, so we avoided them, Kel being a larger Australian breed. There's always something to learn!

*

We continued to satisfy our appetites for live music. The main venue for big international popular live music was the Perth Entertainment Centre; located near the main Perth railway station just off Wellington Street. It was not very old when we were there and we saw some excellent acts, such as Ian Dury and David Bowie on his Serious Moonlight world tour. He came to Perth in November 1983 for three gigs. The ones in Perth were called 'Lets Dance in Perth'. We got tickets the hard way!

We decided the only way we had a chance to see Bowie was to sleep out in a queue at the Entertainment Centre until the morning when they would open up the office to sell tickets. The weather was balmy and we were young, so we set of from Thornley with the dog for company and parked the Falcon in the (free) Entertainment Centre car park. We had brought some basic bedding to lie on and we took our places in the already growing queue.

We didn't have time to bring any supper with us, so someone kept our place while we went across the road and up the hill towards The Old Melbourne Hotel for a burger at 'Hungry Jacks'. On returning, we kept their place for them to do the same. There was a nice feel to it all, lying there looking at the stars in the middle of a big city. As the night wore on, Kel wouldn't settle so I took him back home and bedded him down, then returned to the queue. We did sleep – a bit, but it was something different, and that's always welcome when you're in your twenties. We got the tickets and we saw Bowie.

By now, the Falklands war had started and finished. To be honest, not much attention seemed to be taken up by this in Perth. There were a few Argentinians working at ARC, but there was no animosity that I could see. After all, Britain was a foreign country with a controversial leader, albeit an elected one, to match Galtieri. I think people saw it as the sabre rattling populism that it really was. Besides, even in her declining years, Britain was more than a match for Argentina, so long as the rest of the global community stayed out of it. The irony was that Britain had been prepared to cede the islands to Argentina back in the 1960's, but sympathy for the islanders put paid to that[8]. The Falklands, or Malvinas, remain disputed up to the present day.

*

The year passed by for Sue and I in what we realised was a relatively settled period. We had immersed ourselves in most of what Perth had to offer, going to classical concerts at the Perth concert hall as well as our active night life, tennis and the dog competitions. On the jobs front, I had been to Sydney to look at some machinery due to be brought to Perth. I stayed up all night in my hotel to watch Alan Bond's Australia *11* win the America's cup. Sue flew to Albury/Wodonga in Victoria and Sydney in New South Wales with TUTA, which she loved; seeing all the sights. A big thank you went out to the director, Ted Heagney for taking her with him.

At Christmas there was a bit of a panic when, after a long day's work followed by the works do in the canteen at ARC, I went into the bath house to change and fell asleep on a bench – out cold. Time was getting on, so Sue rang the works to hear that I had already left. Later still, she rang around the Perth hospitals to see if I had been admitted; nothing. Then she drove over to ARC and asked someone to look in the bathhouse and there I was, blotto on the bench. If I'm tired and then I have a drink, I go out like a light. Well, I had won the darts and pool competitions!

In the New Year, we had news that Sue's sister, Jane, who had first introduced us to each other, was due to be married in June 1984, so Sue set out to arrange a visit back to Wales for the wedding. The day of our departure came around. Having put the dog and cat in kennels, Sue was carefully nursing Jane's wedding bouquet. She had it made up specially for her sister. Even though it couldn't be real, it looked beautiful. Sue carried the bouquet in the Boeing 747 cabin. All went well until, on re-boarding at Singapore, she was told it would have to go in the hold. Sue can be fiery when riled and I was cringing as she dressed down the Singapore airlines officials. But they would not yield. I had visions of us spending the night in a modern version of Changi prison!

The wedding went well. It was just the aftermath that went awry. We were at the reception enjoying the celebrations, when Sue's father handed his car keys over and asked her to bring the car to the door, so the wedding presents could be loaded up.

Sue (who hadn't been drinking) went to the car and promptly reversed it out – leaving a nasty dent along the side of the adjacent car. Sue, in tears, asked her cousin in law who owned the damaged car. She replied, "I do, but don't worry, it's only a lump of metal. It can be fixed!" Sue welcomed this wonderful response – all the more since her cousin Brian had just been made redundant! Needless to say, we paid for the repairs. We returned to Perth after our visit, in a sombre mood. We were starting to feel the distance.

Because You're Young

Because you're young no need to care,
if things go wrong for you out there.
The years are on your side, there's time
to put things right, get into line.

Because you're young you can start again,
if you get hurt, if life goes lame.
Don't let your feelings get you down,
shape up and go out on the town.

Because you're young your memories lack,
the force to strike you in your back.
This moment and the one to come,
are all that matter, when said and done.

Because you're young you can go once more,
to find what life is really for.
Only you can open wide that gate,
don't let your setbacks decide your fate.

A passport back

IV

The year of 1984 was upon us, and we were both aware that something had changed. It was as if our adventure had mellowed into the routine life which most people lived. Of course, it had become just that, but it surprised us because our life together had so far been all about the discovery and romance of life in a new country. Added to this was the sense that Sue's homesickness, unlike mine, was getting worse not better. Again, this surprised us because, of the two of us, Sue was the more independent – having left home briefly to work in London when she was single. All in all, there was an increasing pull on us to return to Wales.

This change was difficult for me. I had arrived in Australia determined to 're-invent' myself – to integrate as much as possible into our chosen country. However, we had come here together, and, if necessary, we would leave together. The experiences we shared in this adventure made a strong bond between us. We had become reliant on each other almost exclusively.

On the political front, Malcolm Fraser's protectionist Australia was giving way to the more internationalist Bob Hawke era. One of the more significant internal changes brought about by the Australian Labor Party (ALP) was the introduction of 'Medicare'. This was, effectively, a National Health Service. So the need for private health insurance, in our case with the Hospital Benefit Fund (HBF), would eventually end.

As the end of another year came and went, we were aware that, in March 1985, we would complete our fourth year in Australia. This was important to me as it entitled us to become naturalised – that is to say, become fully fledged

Australians and not just ex-pat permanent residents. I very much wanted this, as I regarded my identity as increasingly Australian. So, in the (Australian) Autumn, we attended the naturalisation ceremony held in Gosnells, just south east of Perth. At a more pragmatic level, I felt (and still do) that the more passportage you have, the freer you can be.

Some of our British friends, who had emigrated at about the same time as us, avoided taking out Australian citizenship. Strangely, some were even a bit hostile to Australians, a kind of reverse POM bashing I suppose. I imagine they felt as though they were being 'unfaithful' in some way, to their mother country. We felt nothing of the kind. I loved the people I left back home, I will even admit to fond reflections regarding the area I lived in. It's just that I felt I could legitimately exercise my geographical freedom without any sense of tribalism. In addition, considering we emigrated for the adventure, we were also making what we considered a wise choice in economic terms. Perhaps this is an early example of the emotion driven self harm which, arguably, later resulted in Brexit.

We each had to swear allegiance to Australia and were duly presented with our certificates of naturalisation. I was honoured and thrilled. I took it very seriously, as Australia had been so close to my heart for much of my life. I always felt that to choose a country and then win its respect is an impressive statement, as opposed to the normal 'accident of birth'. Sue understood this and became Australian with me. Now we were entitled to travel as Australians, so we applied for our Aussie passports.

Sue's passport duly arrived and all was in order. We just had to wait for mine. So we waited – for weeks. Then, suspecting that something had gone wrong, I rang the Passport office to enquire what the problem was. I got what I could only describe as an unsettling reply. The person on the other end of the phone was very patient and said that there appeared to be something on my police file, which I had not declared.

My police file! What was I doing having a police file? You immediately think that there has been a case of mistaken identity – that some criminal's file has been mixed up with yours and you would be barred from the much desired passport. Gathering myself, I racked my memory for anything I might have done; then I remembered – I had been stopped for not wearing a seat belt on my way home from tennis one hot evening. It was only half a mile and I was tired – and lazy, I suppose. Anyway, I put this to the person on the other end of the phone. She said yes, something of that kind would cause the hold up. I had to wait a further week, but then it came – the only ticket out of Australia that I could now accept.

On my work front, Sue was probably pushing at an ever-widening door. My job was becoming more stressful. Allan Carr had left, being replaced by David Westhuizen. The new Plant Engineer was a South African. He was much more amiable than his predecessor and offered me a leading hand roll in the workshop. I was wise enough to know that this could be a poisoned chalice – I sensed that to refuse the job might have jeopardised my position. I felt I was replaceable and so I took on the responsibility. It began well, with my skills base improving with the challenge; for example I could already weld using electric arc equipment but I learned to gas weld using Oxy-Acetylene as well.

Under David, the maintenance team revamped the workshop from a dark oily cave into something a bit more light and modern. I was careful to take on board the opinions of the fitters working with me. We were even allowed to pipe radio music into the shop and we had sundowner barbecues every Friday evening, through the summer!

However, I was conscious that some resentment had crept

into the workshop. After all, I was young, and the mostly ex-pat British crew treated me as 'the enemy' at times. This probably came from their sense of insecurity. So insecurity affected us all, one way or another. This, plus the heavy workload over time, took the shine off the work and I should have looked around for something else. Moving back to the UK was therefore less unattractive than it might have been.

*

No matter how much we try and transcend, there will be a beginning, a middle and an end.

There was much to do. Again, this called for Sue's organisational skills. She tackled the formidable bureaucracy with a will. First, we put the house up for sale. When we had accepted an offer, we set a date for departure. We then arranged for the dog and cat to be taken to the quarantine kennels in Shrewsbury, England, after they arrived by plane in London. They had to stay there for six months. That's a long time in a short life for a dog, in particular. We felt very guilty about this, feeling that we were not 'fit parents!' In fact, we have never owned another pet since.

We then held a garage sale, that's not to say we sold our garage! In Australia, people advertise that they are selling things and then put items out in the garage or, as with us, the car port, to sell to anyone interested. In our case, almost everything – from 'the captains suite' (two settees) to the beds and bedside tables, to our gardening equipment. It all had to go; and it did. The single exception was the dining table, which we gave to Sue's Australian workmate and friend Judy, who said she liked it.

We moved in with Judy, who lived in the northern suburb of Heathridge. Judy was really good to us, as we felt most Australians had been. I doubted very much if migrants to the

UK got the same generous welcome which we had enjoyed. We never got hassled for being 'POMS'. I think this was more common in the eastern states than in the growing multicultural vibrancy that was Perth.

I thought of all the things I would miss about this great country. I would no longer hear the kookaburra call or see kangaroos and emus out in the sticks. I would not miss the flies, but I had somehow got used to them. I knew I would miss the sandy 'soil' of Perth, with its warm temperate climate. Sometimes it is the little things. The 'long ambers' of the Australian traffic lights, and the right to 'undertake' on freeways. Then there is the absence of car M.O.T.'s and TV licences. I would miss the Australian 'strine' which, to my ears, sounded so much nicer than my own Welsh accent. A surprise for me was that I had grown fond of the Australian flora, and I'm not the flowery type. Indigenous plants such as the Bottlebrush, the Banksia and the Wattle bush all meant something to me now. I looked at my Australian passport as though it was an umbilical cord. I would miss my Australia.

The weeks went by and the time came for us to pack in our jobs. Sue pulled the plug first, then I followed. Finally, we sold the faithful Falcon (I can get sentimental that way sometimes). On the day, we said farewell to Judy (no more airport goodbyes), took a taxi to the airport, and we were off; It was May the tenth. This time we were on a Garuda Airways (Indonesia) 747. We had booked a stopover in Bali, so we could enjoy the tropics before heading into the northern hemisphere. We thought to just relax and chill, but we had more fun than we expected!

*

Sigara village was an idyllic resort in Sanur, south east Bali. It had a lovely swimming pool surrounded by pretty 'native' style bungalows. Nearer to reception was a more modest block of two floors with twin bed accommodation; basic but functional. We had an upstairs room, which was nice, as we had a view over the pool. We also saw our first gecko on the wall. One evening we went to a nightclub for a drink and a dance. We met four other Australians there and we chatted on the comfortable seating enjoying the air conditioning. I noticed that a young Balinese was making his way around customers, dispensing items in exchange for Rupiahs.

Sue and I looked again, more closely this time, and noticed that some people were giggling in a pleasant but childlike way. Sue said, "Magic mushrooms." I said, "What?" She added, "I've heard they are about in Bali, they are mildly hallucinogenic, I believe." "I'm not touching that stuff," I said. Sue agreed with me, but we were fascinated nevertheless. The young Balinese came to our table and offered. Two of the Australians from the farming South West had a try. The rest of us declined. Yudi (for that was his name) then went on to offer a service driving us around Bali. We thought about it; then, after negotiating a price, four of us took Yudi up on his offer. We were to be picked up by him in his jeep tomorrow, early.

Now I knew that the Indonesian Suharto regime was basically a military dictatorship. Currently, there was a curfew on, so any trip had to end before that. In the event, Yudi ensured that we all had a great time, seeing parts of Bali that perhaps tourists don't often see. However, it was a bit tight getting back in time. The return journey was a bit racey, with Sue and I feeling a bit like Mel Gibson and Sigourney Weaver in the film 'A Year Of Living Dangerously'!

Through the day, Yudi mentioned that he had an Australian girlfriend and that he planned to move to the land down under in the near future. I felt he definitely had what it took to succeed there. I confess to feeling a little envious that this young Balinese would be enjoying the lifestyle I had just relinquished. The rest of our Balinese break went in a relaxed way. Highlights included beachside massages (very thorough), walks in the beautiful cooler tropical evenings and swims in the pool. After seeing a dead dog on the beach waterside, we decided to skip a sea swim! All absolutely lovely, but hardly a preparation for life in the UK.

As we flew with Garuda, we had to change planes at Schiphol in the Netherlands. This is where I lost my tennis rackets. Baggage transfer couldn't locate them, but promised to forward them should they be found at a later date. I had to be satisfied with that, but I was quite into my tennis at the time, so was a bit disappointed. However, that was nothing compared to how I felt as we descended through the clouds into rainy Heathrow later. I wondered how I was going to shrink back into the small pie that was the UK!

In-Betweening

When still unsure, is there a sign
which way to go; should we toe the line?
It was good fun pushing out the boat,
to see whether we could make it float.

First fully one way, then the other,
Australia first but then run for cover.
Back home once more to take the fight,
to the economic foe, so best sit tight!

But is there life in the wanderers' tree?
Can there be enough left to again break free?
Is it time to relax into fondly dreaming?
Have we reached the last stop in our in-betweening?

The interim years

V

It was like winding back the clock. We agreed that it would be more practical for Sue to stay at her parents house and for me to stay with mine for the time being. So there we were, in our respective little box rooms again, wondering if we had dreamt the last four years! Of course, we took a rental property a short time later; a tiny one-up one-down place in a newer estate on the west side of Cwmbran. Importantly, it had a back garden for the dog, when he came out of the kennel. Everything in our world had become miniature again, and I couldn't help feeling a little claustrophobic – even on the roads, which were narrower. Still, it was mid May. The greenery, which before I left for Australia had been invisible to me, now looked beautiful and lush.

Then we bought a car. This also was small – an old VW Beetle. Orange in colour, I didn't think we would ever lose it in a car park! Next, Sue got a job in her neck of the woods, at the Social Work training centre in Griffithstown (a prophetic choice as it later turned out). I had decided that the days of industrial electricians in modern Britain were numbered, so I took a nine-month full time course to gain a BTEC Diploma in Electronic Engineering. I did this at my old College of Further Education in Pontypool. This was the very same college where Sue had noticed me years before. It really was deja-vu! I also had an eye on any future return to Australia. I thought my chances of getting a job over there would improve with an up to date technical qualification.

In these early months, I had problems coming to terms with what we'd let ourselves in for. It took me a while to adjust and, during that period, I was difficult to live with (I mean more difficult than usual). I did come to accept it though, as my college work took my mind off our return. I also joined a local tennis club and played league tennis through the summer months.

I got work as a barman in a local pub – The Fairwater House, in the area of the same name in Cwmbran; It had a bit of a reputation for being rough. The landlord's name was Jim. He was a big older man who lived above the pub with his wife. He was a fair man, though he did have some peculiar habits – such as calling his bar staff into the office one by one to receive their weekly pay packets. I used to cheat a bit and take my college work to the pub when I was working behind the bar. If it was quiet I'd do a bit of studying on the side.

As with most pubs in the UK, there was a bar room and a lounge area. The lounge was a bit more plush, but the drinks were a few pence dearer. One evening, I was working in the lounge whilst John, the head bar man, was working the bar. I heard a commotion, and went through to the bar, where John was having trouble with a semi-drunk customer. Out from behind the bar, a barman's height suddenly diminishes (the area behind a bar is usually about four inches up on the customer area). Now John was a man in his late forties and stood no taller than me, at about five feet seven. He was out there face to face with the young male customer, looking decidedly vulnerable. I had recently had a closely cropped haircut which, I assume, made me look tougher than I actually was.

Without thinking (I often do things that way), I stepped down from behind the bar and 'commanded' the irate customer to leave immediately. As I did so, I made sure to look him straight in the eyes, as I had heard somewhere that if you don't, it's a sign of weakness. There was a pause (the moment when he is deciding whether to take a swing at me or back down), then he turned and left. John said thanks for backing him up, and I got back behind the bar and pulled myself a pint of bitter!

*

My brother in law, Mark, had been getting increasingly frustrated with the limits of his job as a storeman for a firm in Cwmbran. He had applied for and been accepted into the police training college in England. After he had graduated, he was offered a job as a beat constable by Thames Valley police. He would have to relocate to Burnham in Buckinghamshire, where a 'police house' was ready for him and his family. This meant Julie and Mark, along with Jemma and Sean (now they were up to two children), had to move from their mountainside house in Thornhill Cwmbran, to England.

I thought how this was all an interesting reversal, with Julie making a break for it, whilst I remained home! On the big day, we helped them move, loading up the beetle to the gunnels and going back and forth between the addresses with all the bits and pieces that couldn't be moved until the last minute etc. Happy to say that all went well for them and they settled in their new area, where they live to this day. That's a successful migration!

Meanwhile, Sue was going up to the kennels in Shrewsbury as much as possible to see the dog and cat. Dennis was fine – sleep, water, food, done. Kel however, while healthy enough, was starting to lose the magnificent white brush at the end of his tail. This was the result of the constant rubbing on the harsh concrete floor. Sue made sure he knew he was loved during this period, so that when he finally came back to South Wales with us, he was fine – as was the cat.

The summer months passed by all too quickly and I was nearing the exam period for my course. Sadly, big Jim, the landlord, died suddenly while working behind the bar (I was not in the pub at the time). We were all shocked and saddened by the loss of this gentle giant. After the funeral, his widow decided to let the pub go, so the brewery sent a replacement man and wife team to take over. His name was Mike and he was a bit of a lad!

The pub had a large function room attached to it, which was currently little used. Mike organized for female strippers to appear there every month on a Friday night. I hasten to add that I did not attend. I think the brewery put a stop to it due to complaints from families in nearby housing estates. However, I was sure that Mike was always looking for angles to make extra money. He was just that type of man.

The exam period came and went, and I came away with what I needed. The time had come to start using it! I applied for several jobs; two potential employers showed an interest in me. One was at Abingdon Carpets, who had a factory near Crumlin in the eastern valley. If I took this job, I would be an industrial electrician again. The other was with a company called AB Electronics who were a printed circuit board processing contractor, based in Rogerstone, Newport. This was much nearer to where we lived. More importantly, the title was Process Technician (I could finally make technician grade, after not quite getting there in Panteg). The company was part of the up and coming electronics industry, which was moving into Wales in the wake of the diminishing heavy industries.

I attended the interview at 'AB's' and met Bob Lomas, the man in charge of the Technicians He was very amiable and put me at my ease straight away. I liked him and I think he liked me. I now had to make a final choice. I discussed it with Sue and we agreed that I should move forward and resist clinging to my old trade. So I did!

*

With Sue and I both working and the six months rental coming to an end, it was time to look for a house to buy. This would be our first attempt in the unfamiliar British housing market. The system in Perth was very efficient and customer friendly. Most real estate agents were vying very hard for your business, and so the standard was superb. The British system, if that is what it was, seemed clunky and ill-suited for the purpose. Everything took an age to get done – especially through that ancient privileged group, the solicitors. It was certainly not in the same class as the 'new world' equivalent.

We decided on a two bed cottage near to the Fairwater House, where I had worked as a bar man. This was, as it turned out, a poor choice. The house was OK, though a bit old and in need of a lick of paint etc., but we could have done a bit better with regard to location (it turned out to be the only house we sold for less than we paid for it). You live and learn.

However, all four of us were finally under the same roof together and that felt good. Sue's Dad helped us put a shed up at the top of the garden and generally tidy up. He is a very handy kind of man, and always happy to help.

It was autumn now and, not surprisingly, we found it a bit cold. I used to say to Sue that if you were unemployed and homeless in Australia, you could at least go to the beach and cry yourself to sleep in the warmth. Not so here! I think she saw my point as the temperature fell.

I was working hard at AB's. I found the work interesting and rewarding. I seemed to pick things up OK. The machines were made by global brands such as Universal and TDK (American and German respectively). They were designed to place electronic components into printed circuit boards (pcb's) in the correct place and order, without damage to the components or the pcb's. This is old technology now, but it was quite modern then. It was the tech's job to maintain and program them. There were at least ten machines inserting various components into pcb's, which meant that it could be a bit noisy. However, it was like toy town compared to the steelworks.

After a few weeks, I was allocated a shift and I was back to the twilight life. I have to say though, that the conditions were infinitely more comfortable – and safe – than Panteg, or ARC in Perth had been. In fact, most of the machine operators were female. I had never worked alongside women before and I was warned that they could be just as tough as the men.

A lot of our work was contracted through IBM, the American multinational company. They had a plant in Greenock, Scotland, which we would supply with populated circuit boards for assembling into their business machines. For some reason, it became necessary for us to transport one of our machines up to Greenock temporarily, to be closer to their production lines. This meant that an operator and a tech would need to have a spell in Greenock to operate the machine. I went up with Bob. An operator, also called Steve, had gone on ahead.

Greenock is a long way from South Wales. When we finally arrived, we booked into our hotel and went straight to IBM to check that the machine had arrived OK. To get into the IBM plant you needed an ID card. This was arranged for us and we were led to the Machine. All seemed to be in order, so we went back to the hotel for a meal and some kip. IBM were not stingy with us and we had an expense account to use for food and a limited amount of leisure (beer etc.).

The week went smoothly and we got the work done in good time and order. Bob and I were due to return to South Wales after the first week with Steve remaining, and another tech coming up to Scotland to work with him. Before we left, we went to a nightclub where we met some US service personnel from their installation just over the Clyde from us. Their jobs were to service and maintain the (nuclear) submarines there. They asked us if we would like to come over on Saturday and have a drink with them in their club. We said we'd love to. They said we'd need US dollars when on the site, but they would sort that out when they met us. We went there the next day and enjoyed a warm welcome from everyone. With our pounds exchanged for dollars at the gatehouse, we bought some drinks and enjoyed a delicious meal. Americans know how to put on a party!

*

I don't know when we first realised it, but both Sue and I were coming around to the idea that we should have another crack at Australia. It may have come out of our discussions regarding starting a family. At this point, I must be frank and say that I didn't seem to have the 'paternal bug'. Perhaps that is because I had not finished growing up myself, but who does? Anyway, Sue was starting to feel a little bit maternal since her nephew, Ashley, had been born (the first of two sons for Jane). Sue enjoyed her time with him, taking him out and sharing a little bit of his life.

Now clearly it's different for girls – nature puts a more stringent time limit for reproduction on them. I could see her warming to the idea of having one of her own, but I was against having one in the UK. I felt that we had a golden opportunity (dual nationality) to give a child what I considered to be a great start, growing up as a confident child instead of under the invisible cultural cringe of the British class system.

We seemed to sit on this for a while until, one day, we went to see Crocodile Dundee in the local cinema. I know, it's childish, but it grabbed us and kind of woke up the sense of adventure that had been suppressed for over two years. Sue said to me, 'Shall we try again?' and I, predictably, said yes. The proviso was that we would try and start a family in Australia. We were on our way out again!

In the excitement, we started to organise, as usual. We were getting good at it by now. We were upset that we would have to move the dog back to Perth, but Dennis would remain with my Mother and Father. We put the house up for sale but, in a depressed market, had to accept a low offer. Little did we know that the housing market in the UK was about to go bananas; and us without a property in either country. That's life and, over time, things have a way of balancing out.

This time there would be no Noalimba. We booked accommodation ahead of our arrival, in a hotel right in the Perth CBD; thereby ensuring good transport links until we were sorted. Sue finished at the Social Work Training Centre, and I handed in my notice at AB's. I am always careful to leave an employer on good terms, you never know how the future could turn out. Then it was goodbye, at the doorstep this time, and off to catch the 747 down under. We had been in Wales for just two years and five months.

Electric Arc Furnace 'U' tapping, Panteg.

'Going walkabout at just four years old.'

'...wonderful, except I couldn't swim!'
Putting myself out there. Yugoslavia, c1973.

'...eyes that looked right into your soul.'

Fakarava in the Tuamotus

My Panteg House social club card and my
Cook Islands (Aitutaki) driving licence.

'...in the footsteps of a giant.' Vailima, Samoa.

The view from Tusitala's final resting place, Samoa.
An exhausted Sue in the foreground.

Va'aiga (Inga) Tuigamala. A lovely man.

'...with just a little imagination...'
Mark on 'The Casco' Krabi

A Letter from Australia [circa 1988]

You're there I'm here, it's not good,
though it seems as though you should
be there not here. Your job is mighty,
to help us relocate back into Blighty.
But, by God, it's not easy to try
and squeeze back into that small pie.

The dog misses you, and your walks,
there's silence here now, without our talks.
I hear the red eye late at night,
and consider how to solve our plight.
It's hot as hell this time of year,
I mean of course, not there, but here.

Strange to say, but Perth without you
is empty. It's spaced out anyway, true.
But there's too much room
around me, it sets my mind a gloom.
John in work has invited me
to play some golf at Marangaroo, we'll see.

I hope your mam and dad are well,
but if mine were not, would you tell?
His postie job has kept him fit,
my dad, but my mother, well it hurts a bit.
To think I put her through all that,
just to give up and then go back.

How is my sister keeping? Do tell.
Give her my love, the kids as well.
She's happy there, I'm sure of it,
no need for her to come out here
to find a life, to make it fit.
Something must go wrong, provide a spur.

House prices I hear are ramping up
over there, no sign here yet.
If the land you're looking at
for us, falls through, I'll bet

you'll have to come on back.
You know I won't mind that.

South Fremantle played today,
don't know who won, don't care anyway.
Drove up West Coast Highway yesterday,
I love that run, by the Indian Ocean.
There's no way I'll tire of that,
it's just a simple fact.

I went to Rottnest fishing last week,
with Richard and Ralph, it's not my thing.
We filled a small barrel in no time,
it's too easy, the fish jump on the line.
The day before I went for a swim,
you know the place, City Beach, only me in.

I cycle to work, Cloverdale to Belmont
is not far. It's nicer than driving the car.
I'm playing tennis this weekend,
over at the club, on grass with luck.
The feel of the stuff under my feet,
while I chop at the ball, is very sweet.

Our letters have crossed, I've just received
yours to me, you're coming back.
On Friday week, by Kangaroo,
I'm over the moon, I'm so relieved.
You tell me we must buy a house
quite quickly, prices are going mad.

Over there. It'll happen here
we both know that. But I don't care,
you're on your way. I'm fine with that.
It does however mean this letter
is redundant now. But all the better.

Another go

VI

A week in the Criterion hotel, on Hay Street in the Perth CBD, was a good move. It gave us space to see how the land lay. We rang up a private car seller asking about an old Falcon saloon he was selling. The owner brought it to the hotel the following morning, but it wasn't a patch on our old station wagon. We politely declined and hired a car to look around more widely. In the end, we bought a Datsun (later Nissan) Bluebird automatic – with air conditioning!

I paid a visit to ARC Engineering, my old employer in Welshpool. I met everyone again, including my replacement, Adrian. He was also an electrician from the UK. David Westhuizen had moved on and was running a business in another part of the industrial area. I visited his factory and it was worse than ARC. I realised that whatever I did next, it would not be in such an environment.

Next was work. As usual, Sue scored first, securing a clerical job with The Association for the Blind of WA. I was emboldened one day (probably from Croc' Dundee) and walked straight into the Wellington Street HQ of the State Energy Commission of WA (SECWA). I asked if there were any jobs available for electrical fitters with technical qualifications. A pause; the receptionist rang upstairs, then invited me to the third floor where someone would meet me.

David Gillett came to shake my hand. Explaining that he was the head of the metering department for the Commission, almost there and then he offered me a job! It seems that, at that moment, there was a shortage of technical people in his department. He just happened to be in head office on other business when I walked in. Thus began a marvellous six-year relationship with this organisation.

An interesting perk in Australia was the 'long service leave' system. This was effectively a paid holiday of three months (or half pay for six months) when you complete the service requirement. With ARC Engineering, this period had been fifteen years. With SECWA it was only seven. Yes, after every seven years you got a big chunk of paid leave. Talk about being valued! The best you would get back in Blighty was a carriage clock after forty years. No comparison. I was truly in the lucky country.

Of course, we had made many friends when we were here last. We rang one couple, June and John (we had stayed bed and breakfast with their eldest daughter and son-in-law for a month, before coming back to Perth). They were now living in a suburb south of the river and, as luck would have it, had a caravan in their yard, which they invited us to use until we got ourselves sorted. We took them up on this for three weeks as it gave us time to decide where to rent. They had a dog called Lucy, who was great fun to play with. They also had a swimming pool, so we definitely had a nice break with them!

I remember that John owned a mini van. It worked fine, except that the reverse gear was dodgy. So in the mornings, he often had to push it back off his drive before getting in to go off to work. I helped him on a few occasions. A very laid back man was John. Just the thing in Australia (she'll be right, mate).

By Christmas, we had moved into a rental in the suburb of Cloverdale, near the airport. As usual, it had to have a back yard for the dog, but it was all sand, and one fence was missing. I replaced the fence as the dog was due to come out of the kennels in a few days. The sand was ideal as the dog couldn't spoil the 'garden'. So all 'three' of us would be together again.

I was also lucky to be near Belmont tennis club, in the suburb next door, of the same name; so I joined. It had grass courts, which I loved playing on. I actually won the prize in the club round robin tournament, on grass! Tennis could get no better than this for me.

Then it all started to go wrong. The housing market was suddenly starting to warm up and Sue felt a sudden surge of homesickness and just had to go back. She finished work and we arranged for her flight home. We also prepare the way for me and the dog. I did not hand in my notice – yet. Homesickness is a terrible thing. Some people just get a little sadness, but it doesn't affect their choices in life; I am one of those. Others have it much worse. It distorts life for the inflicted, so that the only cure is to return to the apparent security of 'home'; Sue is one of these. As all migrants have found out, you never know which one you are until you are tested.

Added to all this, when Sue had gone, I tweaked my knee in work. I was now in a pickle. I well remember lying on the couch in Cloverdale late one night, with the dog next to me, listening to the 'midnight red-eye' (overnight flight from Perth to the eastern states) pass over. I was waiting for an operation on my knee. I could not walk properly, but I managed to get Kel to the airport and off back to Shrewsbury.

I have to say that the staff in St Johns hospital, West Perth, were marvellous. They operated on my knee (a dislocation) and sent me off for physio. It was very handy that I had the Bluebird automatic. I could not have driven a manual. I went back with a box of chocs for the nurses when I was mobile again.

*

Sue rang me one evening to tell me that she was looking at some land north of Pontypool, which we could build on. I accepted this, as I trust her judgement completely. However, things took a turn for the 'worse' on this front when she later informed me that the landowner was being difficult. She therefore withdrew. Then the big news: She was coming back!

I thanked God for this major mercy and also that I had not yet packed my job in. Sue said that things were getting serious on the house price front. We knew that the Perth housing market only lagged the UK by a few months, so there were just a few weeks to secure a property before Perth prices went through the roof, as they were already doing in Britain. This was no small thing for us. We stood to have our meagre savings wiped out if we did not act fast. We are good in an emergency, Sue and I. We knew what had to be done and we were going to do it!

I met Sue off the Kangaroo (Qantas) 747 flight from London and, after a night's rest, she was ready for the battle. First we had to decide which area to aim at. Perth is far too spaced out to look for a house all over the place. You have to be strategic. Although my work was based at Belmont, a south/central district, this time we opted for the north. Suburbs in this region were nearer to the sea and we felt we could do with some of that.

Before we could be credible potential buyers, Sue had to get a job. She answered an ad' for a clerk typist at a company called Normet. Sue is good at interviews and she got the job.

Next, which suburbs to look in for our new address. Prices were now starting to move and just a few places were viable. These included Beldon and Heathridge. While I was working, Sue contacted the real estate agents, which were active in the north, to arrange for viewings. In Australia, there has long been a system whereby the vendor gives the agent the house key so he/she can bring buyers to view the properties when it suits them. It's a bit like shopping for a house.

After driving up to Beldon to meet the agent, Sue parked the car and didn't need it again until she had chosen a property. The 'Roy Weston' agent took her everywhere and it took all day (As alluded to previously, Australian markets are generally very customer friendly). There are many migrants in the service industries in Perth, and I have found, through personal experience, that when you give up everything to live somewhere else, you definitely try harder!

There was nothing suitable in Beldon, but my intrepid wife found something in Heathridge, on a street that was within walking distance from a proposed city railway line. Since Heathridge was an hour's drive north of the city, Sue knew that this could potentially be useful. Faversham Way was just off Ocean Reef Road which, predictably enough, went west, straight to – the Indian Ocean; just 10km away.

I had cycled home and, as I came through the door, Sue rang me to tell me the news. Again, I trusted her judgement and first thing the next day, we drove up together so I could see for myself. It would do. A three-bed bungalow (just called a house in Australia) with a semi-ensuite and an atrium type family room. The gardens were reasonably mature and the house itself was only three years old – and not on a corner!

We got a rather large mortgage with the Commonwealth bank. This bothered us a bit until, six months down the track, Sue got a job with the Westpac bank. Talk about being in the right job at the right time! Her position secured the transfer of our debt to Westpac at a more reasonable interest rate (12% instead of 16%) on the bulk of the mortgage, but we also had to have a general loan to cover the rest (18%).

Younger readers will be staggered by the interest rates offered during the 1980's. Although they were uncomfortably high, it should be remembered that the savings rates were also high (if you had any). Thus, our little pile got us 10% with Westpac.

For years after, every Sunday we would go to a little Italian cafe on King Street in the city centre for a coffee and one brownie between us. It may not seem much, but we were happy. You can't buy that. King Street was in a no parking zone but, being a Sunday, I could drive around until I found a parking meter not charging on Sundays. We were good at saving!

In the winter it gets a little chilly, even in Perth. We would often end up parking on Murray Street. During our walks back to the Cafe, we noted that there was a right and wrong side to Murray Street; that is to say, one side was in the shade and the other was in the sun. Needless to say, we always walked on 'the right side of Murray Street'. That expression has stuck with us. To this day, whenever we are on the shady side of a street, anywhere (cold) in the world, one of us will say 'we're on the wrong side of Murray Street'.

*

My job was going wonderfully. Not only were the staff treated with respect, we were also not patronised. There was no sign of the British tendency towards superiority of wisdom and intellect based purely on employment rank. This egalitarianism is a strong feature of Australian life. In general, people are given a 'fair go' irrespective of any pre-Australian cultural baggage.

You could be sitting on a stool at the bar of the local hotel, with just a singlet (Aussie t-shirt) and shorts with thongs (flip-flops) on. Next to you might be someone dressed just as you are, but he could be a wealthy man. You would never know; not by his clothes, or his accent, or his attitude. Another thing missing was sarcasm – the Australians just didn't use it in their straight talking patter. I found the absence of cynicism a little strange at first, since we use it all the time unconsciously in the UK.

Most of my colleagues were migrants, and were around my age. I worked most closely with Karl, from northern Germany. He was a clever man and ran the high voltage metering and testing laboratory in which I was the second technician. Germans cannot hold dual nationality, so when Karl became Australian he relinquished his birthplace passport. That's what I call commitment. Karl spoke very good English; so much so that I asked him one day which language he dreamed in. He said it was still German, but that there was more and more English creeping in!

Llew worked in the general metering section and was another clever man. He was also a really nice guy, and I don't just say so because he came from my neck of the woods – Wales. He came from Cwm, in the valleys. Next was John, also Welsh, from Swansea. John liked football (that's soccer in Aus) and golf; I often went to Marangaroo golf club for a round with him – among the resident kangaroos! There were Scots and other Germans, as well as birth Australians such as Stewart. David Gillett himself was from the south country in England. Everyone realised they were lucky firstly to be in Australia and secondly to work for SECWA. All really nice people.

A trip up North to Geraldton with Stewart? "No problem" I said to David Gillett without hesitation. People doing my job were known as Metering Technicians. Stewart Webb was very experienced in the work. Metering Techs usually got a Falcon panel van to use for work and were able to take the vehicle home. This was a great perk for me as it meant Sue and I only needed to run the Bluebird. My van had three 5's on its number plate, so it was known as the triple 5 van. These vans were not like you might have seen in the UK at the time. They were powerful eight cylinder Ford automatic beasts which could be relied on to take you up and down the massive state of Western Australia.

All state owned vehicles had licence plates with blue letters and numbers on them. This was to show that they did not need to pay the state road tax. Otherwise, the state would be paying the state – a pointless bureaucratic exercise, which some other countries seem to indulge in. As with other countries outside the UK, there was no obsession with the age of the car; that is, no letter or number denoting the year it was made.

We did not take the triple 5 this time. We went in Stewart's van. The trip was for three days; a day to get up there, a day to do the job, then a day to get back. Two nights away. It went well and I went on many more, some as far as Derby, Broom and Kununurra in the Kimberley tropical region (the 'top end'), as well as the Pilbara. Sometimes we flew (there were usually two of us), other times we drove all the way up. That's well over a week away from Perth. We also had to go south to places like Esperance and Albany, as well as Kalgoorlie in the Goldfields, and Laverton in the red centre. Needless to say, I was in my element. I was seeing Western Australia and being paid to do it!

I must confess that, as was the case with most other State Energy Commission employees, I wore the Dinki-di (boy scouts) uniform. I wore the SECWA emblem with the pride that comes from feeling that you are valued. It wasn't compulsory to wear the shorts, but it was so practical; especially in the summers and any time up north. Now it looked strange if someone didn't wear shorts.

Occasionally Sue and I would take liberties. We were young and adventurous so, sometimes, we went together. Usually we would travel with a mechanical tech, in his van. Most often we went with Bev Dawes up north, and Albert Teidki down south. All three of us would bundle into the Falcon (a bench seat with an automatic column change gearbox is so practical). We would drop Sue off wherever we were for the night and go and do the work while she had a look around. This way we were both able to see quite a lot of the state. We have fond memories of these times.

Bev liked a drink, as do most Aussie men (and women). He had a fridge fitted in his van, which was full of beer stubbies. This meant that, wherever we stopped, he always had access to a 'cool one'. Bev was dinky-di (born in Australia) and had served in Vietnam. He had many mates 'up north' who had shared similar experiences in the horror of that conflict. Many were the times when he would 'tie one on' with his mates' after a long drive (he always drove his van), but he was always up and ready to go the next day – seemingly no worse for the wear!

The trouble with the tropics, from Sue's point of view, was insects. Most of all, she hates cockroaches. Of course they are much bigger in these latitudes than in the temperate zones. One night Bev, Sue and I pulled into a motel at Karratha in the Pilbara, on our way up to Kununurra in the Kimberley. As usual, Bev had run a power cord from the van into his room so he could keep his stubbies cool overnight.

In our room, Sue was having problems with the cockroaches and, despite the oppressive heat, had completely wrapped herself in a blanket. All very well as long as the air-con was working, but then we had a power cut! So, unable to bear the heat under the blanket, Sue went out to the van to sleep on the front seat. I slept my usual deep sleep but she told me later that, as she sat there, a drunken couple stopped at the van bonnet and had a blazing row. It seemed so violent that Sue slowly lowered herself down into the foot-well of the van to avoid attracting their wrath. All in all, an interesting night for my wife!

On another journey, we thought we were going to die, as Bev threw the van around the narrow bends in the Kimberley mountains without a care in the world. We decided to take a fatalistic approach. After all, if we died, we would at least be doing what we loved. Cotton wool is no use to young people.

On some occasions I went out alone. One day I was on the edge of the Nullarbor desert testing a piece of equipment. When I had done my work, I drove to the outskirts of a little outlying settlement called Laverton. This was Black Stump country. Looking out on the desert to the east, I remember how perfectly at home I felt in that moment.

*

The phone call had left me in a daze. My auntie Avril had rung to tell me that my mother was ill. She said it might be a good idea to come home to see her. My mother was the centre of our family; of course I would come. I told David Gillett the following day and he offered me six weeks to go home (all migrants dread this call). I booked a flight with Qantas in the city for the end of the week and I was off. Sue would hold the fort in Perth.

I was still in shock as I sat in my plane seat. The Qantas crew were very kind. They had been informed of the nature of my journey and periodically asked me if I was OK.

When I got back to Wales I learned that mam had lung cancer. I did my best to be cheerful for her, but the prognosis was not good and I think we all blanked the horror of it out so we could enjoy what time we had left together. Mam's two sisters, Ivora and Avril, were marvellous with her. They spent hours reminiscing as only siblings can. I did not fall apart but I was not much use.

Mam was told that it was a matter of months. Hearing this, I decided that, after my six weeks were up, I would return to Perth and come back to see mam later in the year. I cannot tell you how difficult such calculations were for me.

Four months later I returned and spent time with mam until the end. David had given me another six weeks to go to see her. When it was over, my dad was shocked beyond words but my two aunties and myself broke down and cried fully and spontaneously from the bottom of our hearts.

One of the most poignant moments for me was the day Julie came down from Buckinghamshire with little Tommy (she now had three children). Dad and I waited for Julie to step off the train and the three of us hugged together in mourning for our reduced family; Tommy on child reigns as I remembered Julie with mam, in happier times. Being so young, Tommy was more protected from the full impact of what had happened. However, Julie later told me that her eldest child, Jemma, took the loss of her Nanna Woods very hard for some years after.

My own memories came flooding back. My parents married in 1948. They had to wait five years for me to arrive, and another five for Julie. Mam nearly died after she had Julie, who was born in the two-bed house in Coed Glas; just around the corner from Cocker Avenue. While mam was in hospital recovering, I was sent to stay with my 'auntie' Nancy. Nancy was a loving, funny, happy, and very strong woman (it's funny how kids can sometimes sense these things). I felt safe with her.

Pneumonia was common in those days and my little sister got a double dose. She was tough though, and came through just fine. There was no central heating when Julie and I were young. Once a week, we'd each be given a bath and were then sent down stairs to stand in front of the blazing coal fire; wrapped in what seemed like a huge, crisp bath towel. Absolute luxury.

Then there was the time when, as a toddler, I was down the garden in my grandmother's house. Mam, nanna Strong (my mother's maiden name) and my auntie Avril were looking out of the window as I picked blackberries from the hedge. One for me, one for Tim (my nan's lovely sheep dog), one for me, one for Tim etc. Only later did I discover that every time I turned to pick another blackberry, Tim would spit the last one out!

My generation were luckier in that respect. When dad came home from work, mam could tell him what his children had been up to. As a family man, he would have enjoyed that. For later generations, with both parents in work, many such moments were lost. In crude economic terms, life for us was low on quantity but high on quality. From little things memories grow. But you need the little things.

The last family holiday we had together was in Cornwall. I was a moody teenager by then. Layla by Derek and the Dominos was in the charts and I did not want to be on holiday with my family. I was young and didn't know any better. Precious.

Many people from the Old Cwmbran community attended my mother's funeral service. The little non-conformist chapel of Pen-Y-Waun, two hundred yards up Waun Road from our family home, was crowded out onto the streets with those who had come to know and love mam. As I sat there, on the front bench with Julie and dad, I recalled my memories of this place. As children, we came to Sunday school and then Christian Endeavour on a Wednesday evening, under the loving eyes of my uncle Arthur (my dad's elder brother) and auntie Mavis – they loved the chaos of little children about them. We were a tight-knit community.

A few days before I was due to depart for Australia, the phone rang. It was Angela, who probably qualifies as my first girlfriend. Now married with children and living in Blackwood, Angela had heard of mam's passing and wanted to offer her condolences. I was very moved by this gesture and told her so. She was an ex-nurse and so would have understood my clumsy attempts to say that mam would have appreciated it. If you are out there reading this Angela, thank you.

My Dad of course needed support. Again, my aunties were wonderful. At times like this, families come into their own. I helped just by being there, I think. I told my dad that he must come and visit Sue and I, when he felt able. He always loved travel and I felt it would give him something to hold on to. On the plane back to Australia, I remembered tearfully our first migration flight and the British lady who was returning to Perth after losing her mum. Now it was me.

During the writing of this memoir my mother's last surviving sibling passed away. Goodnight and God bless auntie Avril. From the very first, to the very last, you were lovely.

*

Life always has to go on and we received the good news that both Sue's parents and my dad were coming to visit us. We had three bedrooms in Heathridge and, being a little nearer the sea, it was not quite as hot, so we hoped our guests would not fry in their bedrooms in the Australian summer.

My father arrived first. He had been taken to Heathrow by

Sue's parents, who would be making the trip two weeks later. As I alluded to earlier, my dad was always a little 'out of touch' with reality. He arrived with his old postman's boots on; he had retired a few years before, but wanted to get the full wear out of them. It was high summer in Perth. After clearing customs, my dad's first words to us were, "It's very hot here." This was not helped by the fact that he also had his long-johns on. It was at least 32 degrees C!

We took one look at his pale slender frame and decided we would set about giving him a more suitable set of clothes to wear whilst in Australia. So, while he took to his bed to recover from the long journey, Sue took his clothes, washed and dried them before putting them away – including the long-johns. Instead of his brown trousers and his beige shirt and off white vest, we gave him a couple of my tee shirts and a nice white pair of trousers, with a pair of my loafers to put on his feet (my dad was roughly the same size as I, or I should say, I am the same size as he). To 'cap' it off, I gave him my panama hat to ward off the fierce sunshine. When he had woken and showered, he dressed and we stood back to examine our work; dad looked ten years younger!

We had two weeks alone with him so I took the time off work to show him around. He was a man of simple tastes, but he had always dreamt of visiting the Goldfields, particularly Kalgoorlie, in the red centre. We arranged to take him there in the car (there are few buses and no intra-state passenger trains in WA). It was an eight-hour journey to Kal. We passed through old farming towns such as Toodyay and Northam before passing through moon like terrain, often alongside the legendary water pipeline, which supplies the Goldfields and makes habitation there possible.[9]

As we approached Coolgardie, my dad, who had been quiet almost all of the way, said, "Are we nearly there?"

Reassuring him that we were, we finally arrived in Kal at dusk. Paddy Hannon's statue was opposite our hotel as we bedded down for the night. Unfortunately, our rooms were above the bar and it was Saturday night. Too noisy for dad, we thought, so we left and booked into a quieter hotel just down the road. At this point, we thought better of taking him down to see the notorious red light district! We all saw the sights and I derived great satisfaction in being able to give my dad one of the few experiences he wanted.

Sue's parents arrived about two weeks after my father. This was another wonderful tonic for us. Mr Taylor had retired from Llanwern steelworks, so he didn't have to go without holidays for a year just to visit us – as he had to on their first visit. Sue's dad was just 55 years young. I have often ribbed him mercilessly since, that he had 'beaten the system' – something that people from the poorer classes in Britain gain satisfaction from.

Our visitors were perplexed by Sue's system of placing a row of thongs (flip-flops) outside both the front and rear doors. This was so that sand would not be transferred into the house. On one occasion, we were all about to leave the house for a day at the beach when Sue's mum noticed my dad was sitting in the car with his bedroom slippers on! We all cracked up laughing, my dad never being quite on the same page as everyone else.

We taught Mr Taylor how to drive our automatic Bluebird (almost always automatics in Australia), so that he could take Sue to work on weekdays and then explore the city and beaches with Sue's mum and my dad. Just like us, they loved the journey down the west coast highway – the route to Sue's workplace in Subiaco. My route, although nice compared to almost any British city route, was not so scenic. My journey to work took about an hour, and passed through some of the older suburbs on Perth's inland (eastern) side.

Both Sue and I worked a nine-day fortnight – that is to say, I had every second Monday off, and Sue had every second Friday off. We worked nine hours a day for the rest of the week to compensate; flexible as ever, the Aussie work culture. This gave each of us a little extra time with our family outside of the leave we took to be with them.

On one occasion, Sue's dad said he fancied a walk to the local shop for a newspaper. Sue and I looked at each other and she said, "Are you sure dad?" He said he was and we pointed the way and let him go. An hour went by and Sue's mum was starting to wonder where her husband could have got to. "He's only gone to the local shop," she said. "He'll be back any time soon," said Sue giggling. When he finally came through the door he was awash with sweat and quite coloured up. "That shop was a long way away for a local," he said. We burst out laughing. Sue and I knew very well that a 'local' shop, or anything else, is not local the way it is in Britain. Everything is on an expanded scale in this huge country.

Mr Taylor got a lot of exercise that week. On the following Saturday, the five of us went to Cottesloe beach, not too far from Subiaco. It was a windy day and Sue's mother had brought an umbrella as a sunshade. She let it go, and off it went. Off also went Sue's dad, in pursuit! Again, the rest of us just doubled up laughing as the chase continued – on to Swanbourne beach, next door. A knowing glance passed between Sue and I; we waited. When he finally returned, Mr Taylor told us that people were sunbathing in the nude on the next beach. Sue's mum stopped laughing at that point! Swanbourne is a known 'come as you want' kind of beach; known that is, to locals.

We have treasured memories of the day we spent on the Peel inlet in the region of Mandura, to the south of Perth. We went in convoy, with Richard and Marion as well as other friends. When we got there we had a look around the town before someone suggested we hire a barge and explore the inlet a bit. "Great," we all said. "Let's do it." So we did. Just one problem; the weather in the Peel inlet can change quite quickly and it did so for us. So there we all were, huddled under the awning at the back end of the barge, with just – you guessed it – Mr Taylor at the wheel, out in the rain, having the time of his life. It was always this way with him and it continues to this day.

*

Time was running out. Sue was now in her mid-thirties. We'd had a busy time of it since we re-emigrated, so our decision to try for a family had been put on the back burner. We could wait no longer. It was time to try.

It is interesting to reflect that to 'plan' a family, is a relatively new phenomenon. Up until the 1960's nature decided such things, broadly speaking. Then, with the advent of the contraceptive pill, control passed largely to women. It was very liberating for women and, I would argue, for men also.

I have reflected on my feelings towards having children earlier; I just did not feel very paternal. For me, children must be wanted and loved – as I was. However, the experiences of my life so far had formed a pet philosophy in me, which went something like this:

All people have a unique set of needs, which as adults, they go out into the world to satisfy, as nearly as possible. In the arena of relationships, partners are selected who appear to offer 'alignment' for each of us. I should add that this process, of course, is not mechanical as I describe, but instinctual and natural. Needs can, and often do, change over time. When these needs do not match sufficiently there is a stress created which can dominate, disrupt or even destroy a relationship. I feel therefore, that it is often not a matter of right or wrong, just alignment. Sadly, children often get caught in the middle of this process of 'dynamic alignment' or, more poetically, 'nature's little trick'. Naturally, I was very keen to avoid such disruption between Sue and myself.

So having children was low on the list for Sue and I – until her nephew Ashley was born. She felt thereafter that she would like to try. Of course, I wanted Sue to be happy, so I supported her in this; so long as it happened in opportunity heavy Australia. Ever behind the curve, I was coming around to the idea of being a parent myself. I felt we had found common ground, or 'alignment', between us.

So we tried. Nothing. We tried for months, still nothing. We tried cycle time techniques and time of the day techniques, more nothing. We consulted a doctor who then referred us to a clinic. This was a private clinic for couples having trouble starting a family. There was no state funded option.

After tests, we were advised to opt for the 'GIFT' program. This is a kind of in-vitro fertilisation; with the sperm inserted into the fallopian tube by surgical intervention. Apparently, most fertility problems reside with the female. Well, it is a complicated piece of kit! My 'end' was OK, so the clinicians said; though it can never be guaranteed, they cautioned, until proof by results!

Sue went through with the procedure. She stayed overnight in the clinic afterwards, but did not look too good to me, the following day. Sue was still groggy from the anaesthetic. I asked her how she felt and she said gently to me, "I don't think I want to go through that again, if it doesn't work." I was almost in tears, but I hid it from her. I just reassured her that there would be no second go; it worked or it did not. From here on it would be nature and not mankind that made the decision.

A week passed by and Sue went for her check-up to see how things were. The news came that a single cell had multiplied just once, and then died. We had achieved just that much. I felt we were smart enough to recognise that nature was telling us something, and we listened. During this period, as with most prospective parents I suspect, we started thinking of names for a child. I liked Lewis for a boy and Toni for a girl. Sue wanted Aaron for a boy but had not decided on a name for a girl. For us, as it turned out, this was one discussion we would no longer need to have.

Mam

Well here we are Mam, after all this,
a mixture of horror, satisfaction and bliss.
Which is which and what fits where,
I'm not quite sure and I don't care.

My adventures have taken me over the line,
to distant places, many a time.
By far the longest stretch of course,
was Australia, living on Perth's clean shores.

You know, I'm sure, I missed you badly,
but I fell in love with Oz quite madly.
I remember you tenderly caressing my hair,
as we shared 'five minutes' in that sitting room chair.

Those moments have always been special to me,
even when I was away on my Australian spree.
Sometimes I didn't listen, but you always knew,
what should be done, the right thing to do.

As I grew bigger and got steadily older,
I came out of my shell and was a bit bolder.
With this, of course, came pain as well,
you felt it with me, I could tell.

We shared our lives as a family,
both Dad and Julie, as well as me.
You were the centre for us all,
as well as around us, you were our wall.

Throughout our time you loved your son,
I felt this warmth, we had much fun.
You must have known I was a dreamer Mam,
that I'd leave you behind, as some sons' can.

You've been gone now for many a year,
but you'll never leave me, not in here.
You'll always be in this heart of mine,
until the man above says "time".

And by the way, I'll add this too,
you're "Mam" to us, "Mum" just won't do.

Going with the flow

VII

Life is a series of natural and spontaneous changes. Don't resist them – that only creates sorrow. Let reality be reality. Let things flow naturally forward in whatever way they like.
– Lao Tzu

"It was probably stress that caused it," said the specialist in Sir Charles Gardiner Hospital, Perth. I had suddenly started having episodes in which my left eye actually 'shut off'. The specialist would not believe me as I explained this to him. Then I described how, if I bent down to touch my toes, my eye would shut off. He said, "Do that now," so I did, and it happened, right on cue. He got quite excited when he looked into my eye with an instrument and saw that I was, in fact, blind in that eye for ten to fifteen seconds; then the sight gradually returned.

After spending four days in hospital undergoing a number of tests, which included a lumber puncture and an MRI scan, the diagnosis was that there was nothing sinister happening. I was just having migraines, brought on by stress. Unusually, I wasn't having the headaches associated with migraines. I was truly odd; but this time, I was grateful that I was!

Sue had said she was worried about her mother's health and wanted to be with her. I knew very well what fear of losing your mum felt like, so I agreed to go back to the UK with her. It turned out to be a serious challenge for me, in both economic and psychological terms, to return to Wales; but the girl I loved was going there, so I was determined to be there too.

My eye had started shutting off after we had sold our house in Heathridge and moved into a rental flat in Jollimont, nearer the city. We stayed there for six weeks, during which time there was a Commonwealth (National) election. It is the law in Australia that all citizens must vote in these elections, so we did our duty as citizens, even though the result would not affect us.

Finally, I had to hand in my notice with SECWA. It was very sad and rather frustrating, as I had been there for six years, and one more year would have given me the long service leave entitlement. You win some, you lose some.

*

It was the northern summer of 1993. I was due to turn forty that August and in those days, forty was the 'hard to get employment' age in the UK. First however, we decided to go shopping for some clothing, which was more suitable for the cooler climate. Then Sue got a job first, yet again. This time as a secretary in a local tie firm (handy if you need a tie, I suppose). I did not know this at the time, but she had sworn to herself that she would do all in her power to try and ensure we would not suffer economically by returning home.

This was one of only two jobs where Sue worked in the industrial private sector; the other was Normet in Australia. She told me that, although she was fairly protected in her office job, she witnessed conditions for the shop floor workers, which were not very pleasant. Nevertheless, she stuck with this job until it was no longer necessary for us.

I saw an advert for a job as a process technician at the AIWA plant near Crumlin. I felt I was more than qualified for it, so I applied. The head of the 'pin in hole' department interviewed me and asked me to work as an operator until a vacancy for technician came up. I should have known this was dodgy as the advert was for a technician, not an operator. However, my lack of cynicism after six years in

Australia left me rather naive regarding the machinations of employers in my home country. I took his word for it and spent the next eighteen months waiting for the tech job that had never actually existed in the first place. We worked a rolling twelve-hour shift pattern, which was brutally exploitative, but it helped me re-adjust to the realities of working life in the UK.

Probably as a result of my early years bullying, I have not been very good at swallowing abuse or obeying blindly in my maturity. I realised, however, that I had to stomach a certain amount of it as a matter of course, in order to keep a job. When the then Tory Secretary of State for Wales, John Redwood, came to the plant to 'inspect' it, we operators were told to stand at our machines as he passed through. The only way I could safely show my dissent was to turn and face the machine and not the politician. As Mandela had shown with his pile of rocks[10] on Robben Island, small steps matter; they matter to me anyway. Of course, it could also have been the Australian okker culture coming out in me!

On the plus side, our two jobs enabled Sue and I to get a mortgage, so we bought a semi-detached house in Goytre, a small village north of Pontypool. There we stayed for six years, with no holidays, until our debt was paid off. This was not the fashionable thing to do in the UK at the time (or even now, I believe); but we had learned an important lesson from the Australians – that a mortgage is a debt to be paid off as soon as possible. This method saved us thousands of pounds. The money was hard earned, but we made best use of it.

Another thing I made best use of was the opportunity to gain a genuine education, as opposed to work related training, with the Open University. The OU is widely regarded as one of the UK's big successes. However, it has been threatened on more than one occasion by Tory governments wanting to thrust a more 'free market' ideology upon it.

I had become quite fed up with ideologues pushing and pulling people into 'necessary' doctrinaire shoeboxes in my home country, and then expecting gratitude for it; arguing basically that it was for our own good. I hoped, for the sake of my Aussie friends, that the trend would not catch on in Australia. Sadly, even though it took a while, it got there eventually; in the form of John Howard's Liberal/Country party alliance, which reshaped the economy there. At the time of writing, Australia has gone from an inexpensive paradise to a cost of living equal to that in the UK. However, shareholders will no doubt be satisfied.

Despite the political ideology, the OU survived and I took full advantage of it. For years I had been very keen on the idea of getting an education, hopefully to degree level, never imagining that it could happen. It was just something I wanted to prove to myself. Was I good enough? Did my eleven-plus failure mean that I was inferior, or even stupid?

It turns out that I wasn't stupid, even though the education system implied it. I studied for six years through the winter months, with summer schools adding as much campus experience as possible. This opportunity came just at the moment when my world seemed increasingly claustrophobic. I was particularly inspired by my first year summer school. Off I went on the train from Abergavenny to Manchester University.

I did my first year in the Arts. We looked at everything from Marx's philosophies to Hard Times by Dickens. I was very impressed with the paintings by the Pre-Raphaelite Brotherhood. This 19th century style of painting stressed attention to detail, and often illustrated a religious or classical story. My favourite painting was 'The Hireling Shepherd' by William Holman Hunt. Lucky me, it was in the

Manchester Art Gallery, so I got to see the real thing!

I graduated with a first class honours degree in the summer of the millennial year, 2000. My degree cost me the princely sum of £2000. It is more expensive now of course, but is still far cheaper than any quality alternative. The Open University is a wonderfully enabling institution, which I fully recommend to anyone wanting a full and rounded education. In case you are wondering, I have not been sponsored by them!

*

A piece of much needed luck! Sue had contacted Bob Lomas, who was now in charge of auto-manufacturing at TT electronics (a renaming of AB's); the firm I had worked for, prior to our re-emigration (I know, but bear with me). Bob said there was a technician job coming up, if I could just wait for a couple of weeks. I waited, and then he asked me into the office and offered me the job. I could have kissed him! I kissed Sue instead.

At long last, life was starting to fall into place for us again. We even started taking a few short holidays abroad. Then, after moving house to Griffithstown in Pontypool, we enrolled in a dinghy sailing course at beautiful Llandegfedd reservoir, nearby. After passing our competency tests we bought a rather worn out dinghy and went regularly to sail back and forth on the 'res'. It seemed a bit aimless to us, to be honest, but we were honing new skills and that is always satisfying.

On one occasion, Sue and I took her dad with us for a sail. All went well until I accidentally gybed, sending the sail flying over our heads and causing the boat to tip over, spilling us into the water. Sue's dad fell in under the sail, but managed to clear it OK (he got wet this time though). The boat then turned full turtle (the mast pointing down).

Sue and I had been trained to right a dinghy. It is not unusual for dinghies to capsize. I went through the procedure of righting the boat and then climbed in, assisting Mr Taylor back on board after. Then we both looked around to find Sue. She was trying to swim towards the boat but was actually moving away from it.

I thought for a moment that there was a current working against her, but it turns out that, when wearing a buoyancy aid, you have to swim on your back, or you go the opposite way! Neither Sue nor I had known this; we do now, lesson learned. Not long after this episode we sold the dinghy, wondering what was next for us.

Looking back, I feel that 'what next' was a very pertinent question. Most people have children and, frankly, such decisions probably get swallowed up with family concerns, so that big stretches of life are decided by default. In this sense there are, broadly speaking, two groups of people in relationships. The people in the 'main stream' group have a period of 'single-hood' in their young lives, followed by a romance, then perhaps marriage and children. Of course, this is a huge generalisation; but one I feel that many would identify with. The second group of people have a similar experience, up to the point before reproduction; and then they pretty much stay where they are, from nature's point of view. 'Child free' couples must, therefore, 'artificially' generate life choices and priorities, which will diverge accordingly.

*

I was now in my late forties and getting a bit fed up with the three shift Monday to Friday pattern we were working at TT's. I had been doing some voluntary work with

Monmouthshire's Youth Justice team, with a view to moving into social work. I applied to Cardiff and Swansea Universities for a place on their Post Graduate Diploma in social work programmes. I was offered a place at Swansea, but the shift work (yes, it was the night shifts) combined with the voluntary work to leave me tired. It was also a longish drive back and forth Swansea. So, for the first time in a good while, I refused a challenge. It was probably a 'better the devil you know' type of thing. Was I getting older? Of course I was, but I don't think I was excited about the challenge or I would have taken it on. I declined the offer, hoping someone who really did want to practice social work, as a vocation, would take my place.

Meanwhile, Sue had left the tie factory and gone back to the council, trying out a job as a medical secretary on the way. She had gradually worked her way up to a level beyond which she could not progress, without further professional training. After doing an HNC at Pontypool College of Further Education, then a Business studies course with the OU, she applied for and got a two-year course in – social work. This was at the University of Wales Institute in Cardiff (UWIC). As I said, she was determined to make it all work!

*

Is it wise? That was the question Sue and I asked ourselves when we thought about committing her student loan money.

One day, I was browsing through the Saturday Guardian newspaper when I spotted an image which focussed my attention. It was a photo taken from the prow of a ship sailing into the Bay of Virgins, in Fatu Hiva, French Polynesia. I read the caption underneath, which was promoting a cruise on a liner/supply boat. The Aranui sails around the Marquesas and Tuamotu islands, delivering much needed goods and supplies, as well as picking up island produce such as copra.[11] All this with tourists aboard. The Aranui is based in Tahiti. Tahiti! That really got my attention.

Sometimes things 'align' in a very clear way. I mentioned it to Sue (remember, I am the dreamer, she is the doer). She said, "It's your 50th birthday in August, why don't we go? We can use my social work student loan." So that is what we arranged to do. We went to STA Travel (originally Student Travel Australia) in Cardiff to book it. They became our 'go-to' company for long haul travel, until they went under due to the Covid outbreak.

First however, we were booked for a sail on a 'tall ship' in early June. The Phoenix was a square rigger which was leaving Penzance in Cornwall on a journey up the Irish sea to Liverpool, for the tall ships festival. We had virtually hibernated from the world for a number of years. It was time to stretch out again. With due regard for melodrama, we called 2003 our 'year of living dangerously'.

"I can't get over the bloody futtocks," said Sue. We were aboard the Phoenix and, along with other members of the guest crew, were climbing the main mast rigging. At the top of the rigging was placed a platform known as the futtocks to sailors. We were required to haul ourselves over this and then go on up to the top. It requires a bit of upper body strength. Sue is very strong from the hips down, but not so much in the arms. She couldn't make it. Never mind; hopefully she would never have to tangle with the futtocks at sea!

Traditionally, there are two shifts, or watches, on a sailing ship. We were assigned to the Port watch. The Starboard watch, we later discovered, included three GP's, off duty and keen to stay that way for the week. The Irish sea was angry.

It is apparently an unpredictable stretch of water, even in June.

The cook was brilliant. She turned out superb food, which many of the crew made the most of. Sue got sea-sick and spent much of the week in her bunk. I was a little better, but was unable to eat too much; what a pity. I did stand my watches though. Four hours on and four off. I loved it, even in the wild conditions.

By the time we were passing the north west coast of Wales the weather improved and the ship headed gently towards the Albert dock in Liverpool. Sue felt better and sat on the poop deck eating what she said was the best apple she had ever tasted (she had eaten almost nothing all week). I had seen the Liver Birds before (Liverpool is the football club I follow), but I was surprised at how different the view was when approaching up the Mersey, from seaward. We all got our things together and said our goodbye's. An unforgettable experience!

*

We could only afford backpacker accommodation on the Aranui. We had arranged to spent three weeks in French Polynesia – two weeks on the ship and a few days either side to look around Tahiti and get across to beautiful Moorea. I am a reader, and I researched the islands so we could better appreciate our time there. Everything from Paul Gauguin, the French painter who came to live in the islands, to Herman Melville's 'Typee' (he also wrote 'Moby Dick') and on to the Kon-Tiki expedition; led by the academic and adventurer Thor Heyerdahl. The Norwegian is a big figure for me, regarding the South Pacific.

Heyerdahl's expedition of 1947 set out to prove that Polynesians could have originated from the Americas and not South East Asia, as was conventional thought at the time. He was later proved wrong, but I just loved his romantic Errol Flynn like daring. In fact, recent DNA tests have indicated a link between Peruvian natives and Polynesians, though the first Polynesian colonisation did originate from South East Asia.

Heyerdahl and five other Scandinavians (five Norwegians and one Swede) had set out on a self-built balsa raft, tied together with natural fibres (I remembered fondly the canal rafting we did as kids). They sailed the Kon-Tiki (the name of an Inca sun-god deity) from Peru for 5000 miles across the ocean to Raroia reef in the Tuamotu islands, where the raft finally broke up (the Kon-Tiki is in a museum in Oslo and is on my to-do list to see). During the journey, if any of the crew had fallen off, the raft could not have turned around to save them.[12]

In 1937 Heyerdahl, and his new wife Liv, had gone to live the natural life on Fatu Hiva. They built their abode from natural materials found in the jungle around them and lived a life we might consider as paradise, for a time. One way and another however, it all went wrong and they had to evacuate after a year, having gone through hardship in the process.[13]

For me, it doesn't matter that Heyerdahl got it wrong, in both these quests. He had put himself out there; he had tried. He is therefore one of the adventurers that I admire.

*

We arrived on the Air New Zealand flight from LA to Papeete at the crack of dawn. Outside Faa'a airport, we caught a Le Truck 'bus' (it is really just an open sided van with bench seats running down both sides) to our hotel, where we dropped onto the bed for a long sleep. I don't

124

know what it is about Pacific and South East Asian hotels, but they always seem to have large beds!

"This has to be one of the most expensive places on earth," I said to Sue, as we looked around the shops of Papeete. "How can people afford to eat here?" she said. Broadly speaking, There are two major groups of people in Tahiti; Polynesians and a smaller group of Europeans, most of whom are comfortably off French. The Polynesians tend to be poorer, of course.

After searching around, we found the open market area, just behind the road running past the quay. Here, plenty of good food was available at better prices. Also, the administration subsidised essential food stuffs such as bread. Tahiti is not financially viable without assistance from the French tax payer. Almost everything has to be brought in from abroad, hence the high prices.

For the first two days Sue and I regularly went to the local petrol station to buy a baguette and a tin of tuna. On the third day we got on the ferry for Moorea, long a place I had wanted to see, and it did not disappoint. We hired a couple of push bikes and set off around the island, having booked a Chez; a hut to sleep in, half way around. We set off to enjoy this beautiful corner of the world.

We were approaching the Chez as the sun was just setting. I remember the magnificent colours of the peaks on the land side of the track, with the Pacific Ocean on the other side. We had just enough light to get into the hut. Thinking that it would be unwise to leave the bikes outside, we brought them in with us. The bed, the bikes and us; no room for any more!

We're hungry now of course, so we look around for somewhere to get food. Up the road and down, nothing. The only hope was an unlit beachside bar next door to us.

Thinking they would open for customers any time now, we picked a bench at the ocean side and waited to be served. No one came. We decided to look around the sides of the building to see if we could attract attention. We found a kind of hatch in the wall where a few people were standing, being served some kind of fast food – perhaps curry. That will do, we thought, getting desperate now.

At last our turn came to be served. The tropical night was pitch black by now. We ordered and received our curry and rice, a concoction that was more liquid than substance. Having paid a kings ransom for our victuals, we went back to our lovely perch by the ocean and then realised we had no implements with which to eat the curry. By now we were not at all fussy and I lost my rag a bit and stuck my fingers in the goo and put it in my mouth. Sue looked at me with amazement and just burst out laughing. She then did the same. It was ridiculous, and that was why it was funny. A good example of things going wrong in the best possible way!

Up early and on the bikes. We had opted to go 'clockwise' around the island, so now we were approaching the two beautiful inlets, which bite deeply into Moorea's northern coast. First came Opunohu bay, which we thought was lovely. Then came the famous Cooks bay and we were not disappointed.

At the head of this stunning bay stands the village of Paopao. We stopped here for a cool drink and a bite to eat. From this point we could see the full extent of the inlet, all the way out to the fringing reef. "Breathtaking," we both said. As we were sat on the bench outside the snacks bar, a man approached us and asked where we were from. We told him, then asked his origins. His name was Nicki and he was Japanese. He and his wife had retired to Moorea years before, but she could not settle and went back to Tokyo.

We thought for a second about the contrast between one of the busiest, crowded cities on earth and Moorea. A big change so late in life. However, Nicki had stayed on and, apart from a little loneliness, was very happy. He liked to talk to foreigners to practice his English. We were happy to oblige as we sat there chatting like old friends who happened to be in one of the most beautiful places on earth! Finally, we said our goodbyes, but not before exchanging addresses so we could write postcards to each other. Back home we got used to the cards dropping through the letterbox with 'Pacifique Sud' on them. (We corresponded for years after, until Nicki suddenly stopped sending; so we sadly assumed that he had died). This encounter was a reminder to us that we continue to meet lovely people on our travels.

Back on the bikes but, before we had cleared the village, Sue fell off and almost went under the wheels of one of the few cars on the island at the time! That's travelling for you; never knowing what's going to happen next. We then settled into the final quarter of the journey. This section took us up a steep-ish hill, which I managed to cycle, but Sue walked up gently; sensible girl, in the tropical heat. We then got to coast down the other side whilst taking in the magnificent view of the reef on this, the north east side of the island.

The ferry was in when we returned our bikes, so we quickly boarded and sat down. It was then that I noticed that I still had the locks, which were provided with the bikes in my backpack. Without thinking, I dashed back off the ferry and over the road to the hire shop, handed the locks in and dashed back, just in time. I sometimes forget things!

*

"Come aboard," called a voice with a distinct Californian accent. Ron, for that was his name, was already firmly ensconced on the Aranui and, seeing we had luggage at the gangplank, naturally assumed we would be shipmates. This friendly welcome was magnified tenfold when we were told by the staff that we had been upgraded to a cabin, all of our own! This was the Aranui II. I had wanted to get on the original one, but it was decommissioned just before we had arrived. So the Aranui II was virtually brand new (At the time of writing, the Aranui V is in use).

Once all the guests were on board and the freight loaded, we were off, out through the reef pass and then north towards the Tuamotus. We were in luck in more than one way. I am not a 'foodie' but, after our meagre diet of late, we were happy to hear that the Chef was French and we were in for a culinary treat. Another piece of luck; we had on board an expert on Pacific archaeology, Professor Charlie Love, (he had actually met Heyerdahl), who would give lectures and help to open up the experience to come.

Cultured black pearls were bought for Sue, her mother and our sisters Jane and Julie, as well as Jemma. We got them on Takapoto in the Tuamotus. On we went to Hiva Oa in the Marquesas islands where we visited Paul Gauguin's grave, set atop a hill so that the old artist could appreciate the magnificent view for eternity. We also went to Anaho Bay, one of many beauty spots in the islands. This was the place of which Robert Louis Stevenson (another adventurer I admire) wrote "Of the beauties of Anaho books might be written."[14] He called there on his travels in the schooner, 'Casco' in 1888.

Next we called into Fatu Hiva, at the main settlement of Omoa. Here, after looking around the village and chatting to the locals, some of us (including me) took a hike over the mountain to Hanavavae. Sue went around on the Aranui to enter the famous Bay of Virgins. The hike gradually turned into a walking race and I joined in wholeheartedly. I'd even brought along my hiking boots for just such an occasion.

All the walkers were given refreshments at the top of a hill, which were laid on by some of the crew of the Aranui. Then I noticed one or two of the younger hikers quietly peeling off to continue the walk, so I went too. It was a wonderful view from start to finish and I thought how Thor and Liv had made a great choice in selecting this barely settled island for their attempt to return to nature. I finished second incidentally, just after a Frenchman. We all enjoyed it and were bathed in sweat. We grabbed a hosepipe and soaked ourselves where we stood!

From this southern group of islands we went to the main island, in the northern group, Nuku Hiva. Compared to Fatu Hiva, this looked like civilization. We went over another mountain, this time in a 4x4 driven by Thomas, a Marquesan, to see the Typee valley, made famous by Herman Melville in 'Typee'. We also climbed to a site where Tiki's and Paepae stood; relics of indigenous religious structures, before western society converted the inhabitants to Christianity.

We always had interesting discussions during the evening meals on the Aranui. One of the guests, Bernard, was a surgeon and had been particularly free with his knowledge, and opinions, about all manner of topics. One evening at the dining table Bernard (emphasis on the *ard*) was again offering us his wisdom. When he had finished, Ron said "Bernard, is there *anything* you don't know about?" This straight speaking retired Californian carpenter had said what the rest of us were thinking!

After visiting one or two more islands we left the Marquesas and sailed south, calling at Fakarava in the Tuamotus before heading back to Tahiti. The week had been memorable for us both and we had made friends with other guests. Ron the Californian exchanged letters with us for some years before, once more, they stopped and we sadly assumed the worst.

We still exchange Christmas cards with David Rainbird, a retired teacher from Liverpool.

We felt privileged to have tasted the delights of French Polynesia and left with no regrets for having blown Sue's student loan on the experience. It is a fact that we have never regretted spending money on seeing and experiencing places and cultures previously alien to our own. We were looking forward to the next opportunity!

In the September we moved to Llangybi, a village near Usk in Monmouthshire. As usual, I was having trouble with night shifts at TT's. In Griffithstown it was too noisy, with traffic out the front and, just the other side of Panteg House cricket pitch at the back, there was a school. We felt that a peaceful country location would help, so we moved, yet again. I had also started getting help from a consultant in Bach's flower remedies, in Blackwood. Mr Tillott was a kind understanding man, who had a remarkable calmness about him. I would go to him when I needed help, for years to come. Sue and I also started meditation classes at the Lam Rim Buddhist retreat in rural Monmouthshire. Even with all this, I was still having to pull into a lay-by on my drive home after nights, because I would have fallen asleep at the wheel otherwise.

We went even further with this nights thing, taking breaks of a week at a time in the Canary Islands during winter months, so I could miss my week of nights and cut down on our Seasonally Affected Disorder (SADS) at the same time! We had always been happy in Tenerife, having spent our honeymoon there in July 1980.

I had a scare when my dad became ill on a visit to Scarborough, in the North of England. He was brought to the local hospital where he recovered enough to go home. Home now was in Thornhill Cwmbran, where he lived with his new partner, Doris. They looked after each other and I am sure both their lives were enhanced by the relationship. I used to cycle up to their house on my days off to see them and have a cup of tea and a chat.

*

We were aware that we had changed our direction of travel, from back and forth Australia (wet willies) to a broader platter. The next opportunity (excuse) for a trip came in the form of Sue's 50th birthday in 2007. Being in January, Sue's birthday fits in nicely with our eagerness to escape the worst of the British winter. This time we called it our 'Under Capricorn' trip.

The itinerary read as follows: South Africa, spending a week in Cape Town (this had long been on Sue's to do list); Perth and south Western Australia, to catch up with our friends; across to Cairns to scuba dive on the legendary barrier reef, dropping in to Uluru on the way; then up to 'the arsehole of the world' as dinky-di's call Darwin; before flying to Bali for a well earned rest!! By this time Sue and I were each deaf in one ear and I was limping from a sore toe. Eight days later, we left the southern hemisphere once more to go back to Blighty. It had been a month well spent.

There were a few notable occurrences during the trip. One was in Cape Town where, having hitched a ride on the back of a 4x4 truck (Sue rode in the cab with the friendly South African), we were dropped off at the Cape Town Yacht club. We had read in the hitchhikers guide that, every Thursday, the club went racing in Table bay and guests were welcome. It was Thursday, so we went in and met everyone. We were made very welcome and invited to help crew Summer Love, a nice 42-footer, which looked like a dream and sailed even better.

We didn't win and I haven't a clue who did, but it mattered not at all. We all had a barbecue (what else?) afterwards with plenty of inward lubrication! When we returned from our trip, we sent Welsh wooden love spoons to the owners of Summer Love, Rob and Lynette, as thanks for their hospitality.

We went to Simonstown in third class on the train, which was regarded as a bit risky by the locals. We didn't let that stop us, but took the precaution of pairing up with a couple of young Korean students who were also making the trip; safety in numbers. Another precaution I took was to hide our money in my sock! During the journey, a woman wearing local clothing was sitting opposite us and she kept glancing our way. We wondered what this might be leading up to. Just before she got off, she went up to Sue and placed a piece of paper into her hand. Sue looked at the paper on which was written a moving religious text. Before Sue could thank her, she had gone. There are lovely people all over the world; all you have to do is go out and find them. This one came and found us.

We could not leave South Africa without visiting Robben Island. This is the infamous place where Nelson Mandela was incarcerated for 18 years of his life. The man was an example to us all and had not a shred of bitterness, despite his ordeal. Our guide went by the name of 'Spark' and had been a prisoner himself on Robben Island for seven years, during the struggle for democracy. This was in the face of governments around the world, including Mrs Thatcher's, lending support to the apartheid system using the 'moral' argument that the ANC was a terrorist organisation.

The cells were 2m square and, despite the latitude, got very cold in winter. Mandela's cell was number 5, in Block B. Coming away, we felt how people can sometimes defeat seemingly hopeless odds. Respect! Then it was back to

Johannesburg to catch the Kangaroo to Perth.

*

In Western Australia we looked up old friends, hiring a car to do so. The accident happened as we were on our way west to Bunbury, having visited friends in the farming country. Passing through the forested area between Nannup and Balingup we suddenly saw an emu jump out of the bush on the opposite side of the road. An oncoming ute (utility truck) narrowly avoided it, but I could do nothing to prevent the bird hitting our bonnet. The bonnet caved in and blood flew everywhere. We were in shock and, seeing the emu lying in the kerbside, knew that it had to be put out of its pain. The ute had stopped and the driver came over the road with a shovel to despatch the unfortunate animal.

We were extremely upset to think that we had caused this, even though I knew there was no way I could have avoided it. In my years of driving throughout WA I had never before hit anything. It was February the eleventh 2007.

In Cairns we went to the Daintree forest up towards Cooktown. We took a boat down the river, seeing crocs on the banks as we went. Later in the week we went out on the reef and did some assisted scuba diving (our first time). A wonderful experience but I think this is where we both picked up temporary ear problems. On to Darwin and our worst backpacking accommodation yet! Never mind, we visited an aircraft museum out of town. We did the journey both ways on foot. By the time we got back we went into a shop and almost begged for an iced cream. We were just short of the price, but the lady took one look at us and gave us the iced cream anyway.

We decided to go to the yacht club (we always seemed to be attracted to yacht clubs on this trip) in Fanny Bay. We sat outside (obviously, in the tropics!) with our evening drinks in hand when suddenly the heavens erupted with thunder and then – deluge. We got wet but it never seems to bother us near the line (the equator).

Bali. Beautiful relaxing Bali. This place was becoming familiar to us, having been here a couple of times previously. This time we stayed at a beautiful family run hotel, which had a pool. Bliss! Eight days later we crossed from 'Under Capricorn' to the northern hemisphere, stopping briefly in Singapore, on our way home. A never to be forgotten experience, again. We felt we were very lucky people.

*

When I heard the news, I was at work. I said to Sue over the phone, "I'm an orphan now." I don't know why I said it; I was nearly fifty-four, but it just hit me. 'Goodnight and God bless' dad. He had often said this to his children in happier times. Dad may well have seen this coming. He and Doris had married not long before, which gave her a little more financial security. He was that kind of man.

We had found out that dad had coeliac disease – a kind of wheat allergy which, among other things, stops the stomach from absorbing nutrients. It is transmitted genetically, so Julie immediately got herself and her children tested. The kids were fine but Julie had it. This helped to explain a lot and her health came on in leaps and bounds when she was put on the appropriate diet.

I was in the clear. We suspected that my mother also had it, as her symptoms had been similar. I had a test every year for a few years to make sure it hadn't 'switched on'. I also broadened my diet at this time. I had been a pesco-vegetarian for eighteen years up to this point.

The sad news continued and, after a long and courageous battle with illness, Sue's mother died the following year.

Just to finish off what had been a bad period for us, I was finally made redundant from TT's in 2009. I had worked there this time for thirteen years.

Lock in and lock down

VIII

Oh lovely lovely Tropic Breeze,
cast your delight upon my ease.
Blow strong and deep within my soul,
for I need you to make me whole.

It was probably a mercy in my case. I had been struggling for some years and TT's had become a less than happy place to work. There had been two previous tranches of redundancies but I had dodged them, being able to work with both the latest method of populating printed circuit boards, Surface Mount chip (SMT) technology and the obsolescent Pin in Hole equipment. It also helped that I was electrically qualified.

The process technicians (including me) were required to work across a number of machine manufacturing platforms. As well as the pin in hole machines of the American Universal and German TDK types, there were now SMT machines which were supplied by the Japanese Fuji company and the German Siemans firm. Ancillary equipment was procured from other suppliers. This required flexibility from us, but was quite stimulating and challenging; all of which I found enjoyable during the earlier years of my time with TT's.

However, the section manager, Bob, (who had employed me) had been 'let go' a few years previously, and this had probably kicked off my gradual alienation from this work environment. The atmosphere became one in which we were always aware that the firm was fighting for its survival.

TT electronics did survive however; I believe much of the credit for this must go to the new general manager at the time, Graham Davies. He moved us away from our dependence on IBM, taking contracts from a greater range of customers to better insulate us from market instability.

In the end, the increasingly video screen centred new generation of machinery favoured those who were a bit geeky and enjoyed the computer games format, which was evolving. This was not my cup of tea. I prefer the real world to the virtual otherworldly way of doing things. I took a couple of courses in Maths and technology with the OU to try and stimulate my enthusiasm, but it would not come.

I have always been that way. Sitting in my local pub thinking what to do, I would always choose darts or pool. There were others who went to the 'one armed bandit' slot machine next to the bar. Then, placing a pint on the top, they would spend the evening making love to it! As I have said earlier, gambling is not my thing.

To be fair to TT's, I was treated in a proper manner financially. Mike, the section head, was a decent man and I took away a redundancy package equivalent to about twelve months pay. Sue and I used some of it to reduce our mortgage to a negligible amount. We also replaced our ailing Rover saloon (we had bought it from Sue's dad six years previously) with a lower mileage Vauxhall Corsa. I then had a moment of weakness and bought my Mazda MX5 (second hand of course). I am still driving it now, over thirteen years later.

I had a good run at TT's and have no complaints. As referred to previously, it is a truism that everything in life has a beginning, a middle and an end. The time spent there had helped get us through, financially speaking. Solving the economic problem is, of course, the pre-occupation of most ordinary people. Up to this time, I had always left my job, moving on for one reason or another (usually to change countries!). This was the first time that my job had left me! As with the steel works, I would never work in the electronics industry again.

A word about management techniques in the UK at the time. On several occasions I have had to suppress my resentment at being micro-managed, sometimes by people who know very little about my job. I have always felt that there is an implied lack of trust in this. If you select someone to work for you, then you should at least back your judgement with a level of trust. I therefore see the micro-management approach as misguided and demotivating. For me, it is a failure of management. I had not seen much of this at either AB's or later, TT's; but management theories are sold to firms just like any other commodity, and can become fashionable. To be honest, I don't think the UK has managed to move on from negative management practices and this may be one reason for the country's poor productivity rate.

My employment history as a skilled tradesman in the UK is coloured by structural job insecurity. This is common in the British industrial sector. The politics of the free market were particularly dominant in the closing decades of the 20th century (there's that ideology again).

Fear of closure had also long been a fact of life at Panteg, but it had survived in the post war years by converting to stainless and special steels manufacturing. By the 1980's however, the steel industry was becoming increasingly global, promoting competition and stimulating new rounds of more efficient technological innovation; Panteg struggled to compete. A little later, many of my old workmates were offered redundancies or transfers to the much larger Llanwern steel works in Newport.

My old shift mate John 'concrete' McGrath was one of those who elected to go to Llanwern. He later accepted redundancy, I believe, and took up the tenancy of a pub in Talywaun. Sue and I went up to see him and his wife Crid one evening and had a chat about old times over a beer (or two). He was a natural pub host but, as he himself conceded at the time, he was a bit too near the grog in that job!

Sadly John, along with many of my other workmates in Panteg, is no longer with us. Sue will always remember his almost toothless smiling face as he walked towards her in Pontypool one rainy day; he was carrying a bag of fish and chips under his coat to keep them dry from the rain. John was a man who was easy to like. That was the last time she saw him.

The old RTB's, with all its history and traditions, was eventually brought to an end in 1996, having been sold to the private sector some years before.

*

What to do next? I applied to a Welsh government scheme, which offered funding to retrain people who were made redundant. I had decided to learn to drive lorries and articulated vehicles (again). I reasoned that at least I would be 'out doors' and relatively free from what I call the 'perfect police'. As mentioned above, these are people who's sole job seems to be to make others' lives a misery. Almost every work environment has them. I felt the worst was at AIWA, where every moment of the working day had to be accounted for and trust was non-existent. That could have been, however, just the way that my fellow Welshmen in the top jobs preferred it. Promoting the search for never ending efficiencies, this process can squeeze the humanity out of people in any type of work.

To their credit, the Welsh government, like many European countries, has always embraced a more compassionate (and

139

less ideological) 'social democratic' outlook. That is to say, where possible, they use the market for the benefit of people, and not the other way around (although, since Brexit, the Welsh government may now be out of tune with their own population). Parts of Wales were regarded as 'poor' by European standards, so received funding from Brussels for projects to help regeneration after the years of de-industrialisation. (Despite promises, the current UK Government do not intend to match this support, never mind exceed it.)

So I got my funding and trained to be a truck driver. I passed first time for the 'artic' ticket, but had to re-sit my rigid lorry test after I was cut up on a roundabout and failed to respond quickly enough. Now I was qualified to drive trucks in both the UK and Australia and, as with Perth, I didn't get a job doing it! Unfortunately, there was no work for truckies in the UK at the time (how things change).

I found some work with a nursery, driving children back and forth, for about a year. It was only part time and the money was very poor, but at least I was out-doors, driving and looking after the mini-bus, which was used to move the kids about. Not having children, I found this work a refreshing change. I got on well with them and I think they took to me. We used to have a 'tractor alert'. We would be travelling through the beautiful Monmouthshire countryside on our way to or from the nursery, when suddenly one of them would spot a tractor and call out to us all. It was the kind of fun I had not experienced before, and I enjoyed my time working with them.

However, the nursery was hitting hard times and I was laid off and then restarted later. I thought it best to look for other employment and found out through Sue that they were looking for a 'Meals on Wheels' driver in Monmouthshire. I applied and got the job. A new beginning and a new challenge. Instead of working with the youngest people in society, I would now be working mostly with the oldest!

For a while I carried on doing both jobs. They dovetailed quite well, although, as most who have done it I'm sure will agree, two part time jobs is harder work than a full time one. Then the nursery work finally dried up and I settled in to delivering meals for a living.

I found that the service is more than just a meals provider. Monmouthshire, in particular, has quite a large rural community. People are scattered about the county in small groups and are often quite isolated from everyday contact with others. The service personnel are human beings, so just the fact that they see lonely people every day, and chat a little, means a lot to many people. No, it's definitely not just about the meals. All in all, 'meals on wheels' is a people centred service and not a profit driven one. It is surely true that the way we treat our old and vulnerable people is a sign of how civilised we are. I was still learning.

*

'Let's go back-packing in Thailand' I said to Sue. As usual, I had been reading and dreaming about somewhere else to go, this time for the February and March of 2010. So we booked a room there. Yes, it was called 'Somewhere Else'. It was a collection of humble beach huts run by local people on Koh Lanta, in Thailand's beautiful Andaman Sea chain of islands. This was not five star stuff, or any star stuff, but we didn't want that, just the location, which was right on the beach.

We planned it carefully. We would fly to Bangkok and look around there, before going south by overnight sleeper train to Phuket where I had read there was a float plane which could take us up to see the Andaman from the air. Then we would make our way to Koh Lanta to spend time on the beach (of course), before using the ferries to look at some of the other islands.

It was a nice combination of the planned and the spontaneous, and most of it worked out really well. We couldn't get a train south as it was booked out for the Chinese New Year, so we flew to Phuket instead. There we found that there was no float plane currently operating, so we headed off by commercial mini-bus to Koh Lanta. It was exactly what we had hoped for, as were the other islands. I knew then that we would be regular visitors to these islands in the winters to come.

Two other islands in particular, are worth mentioning. The first was Koh Bu Bu, a tiny island you could walk around in half an hour. It was family owned, and it was an island paradise. Lights out (generator off) at ten pm. We felt very close to nature.

Walking clockwise around the island with the sun beaming down, we came upon a lovely secluded beach. Looking around us, we could see no-one about, so we got naked and took a lovely refreshing swim. A little later, we were in the grip of nature (think Deborah Kerr and Burt Lancaster in From Here to Eternity). Then, suddenly, Sue tensed up as she sensed we were being watched. She was right. Looking carefully, I spotted a large monitor lizard in the bush, which then scurried away. Spontaneously, we both burst out laughing at our being 'discovered'.

The second island was Koh Seboya, where we hired a lovely hut for a few days (a little more grand, this one). It was here that Sue had her 'peeping tom' shower (a kind of semi-outdoor arrangement in these parts). Looking up, she was startled by a Tokay (a large Gecko type creature) in the roof beams looking down at her! What is it with Sue and members of the lizard family? From then on, our lodger patrolled the beams above our bed, serenading us with his call every evening. We mentioned this to the bungalow owners who said that they knew about him. "It is his home" we were told. Buddhists avoid harming fellow creatures. We felt the same.

Geckos are everywhere in these islands. We had one in our hut in Somewhere Else. Every evening he would make his unique call several times. It is a funny call, a bit like 'ock o', and we laughed a lot at our Geck. We were told by some Thais (who are quite superstitious) that if a Gecko calls seven times in a row, it would bring you good luck. Yes, we counted, but three or four was all ours could manage.

We had intended to look at an island called Koh Jum where there were tree house huts, but we went instead to Koh Phi Phi. This was where the blockbuster film 'The Beach' was made. It was a wonderful place; though, when we went, it seemed to be suffering from over exposure to tourists.

We then made our way up to a place called Surat Thani, where we embarked on the sleeper train back to Bangkok. We managed to see the Grand Palace before it was time to take the big bird (as I've said before, I love the 747's) back home. It had been another wonderful trip to the tropics. Unlike many people, I found that I enjoyed Thailand's hot and humid conditions and Sue barely broke sweat. In the very basic beach huts we stayed at, there was no air conditioning and not even a fan to cool us down after the generator was shut off for the night. We probably became acclimatised. We were definitely hooked!

We became regular winter visitors to Thailand. Most of the time we stayed in beach bungalows in Koh Jum. We didn't stay in the tree huts as it was a precarious journey out of the trees if you wanted a pee in the pitch black nights (no light pollution). The generator would shut off at 10pm as usual and we would be on candles or torches through the night.

We always met interesting fellow travellers on the islands. Many came from Scandinavia (they often brought their kids with them) and elsewhere in mainland Europe, as well as the UK and the US. We occasionally met Aussies and Kiwis, those great travellers from down-under. The local people have a peaceful elegance about them which may be due to the deeply Buddhist element of the Thai culture. On the islands there is also a strong Moslem presence. On Jum, for instance, the local village is predominantly Moslem, and has its own school to support the Moslem way of teaching their children. Nowhere did we witness any animosity between belief groups. All are wonderfully tolerant. A lesson perhaps for Western cultures.

On our way to and from Jum on the ferries, we would stay in Krabi on the mainland. Krabi has no beach to speak of, but it has local culture and it grew on us. This is where we would get a famous Thai massage to relax our muscles from the stiffening northern winter. We also loved eating at the local outdoor market near the river. We were always amazed at how the Thais were somehow able to cook amazing healthy food with only portable equipment and no electricity. We loved it all and have many happy memories of these years.

One evening, we noticed an old man dining at the outdoor market. His dress suggested that he had very little in the way of worldly goods. He seemed to be speaking a combination of French and Thai. We saw him again regularly after that. I formed the impression that he was an ex-pat who had retired and was living out his days in Krabi. The staff at the market seemed to know him well and were very considerate towards him. My imagination set off again. I decided that he was alone in the world. Compared to retirement in cold inhospitable Northern Europe, he was enjoying the beautiful Thai culture and climate until his end. It was the sort of thing that Somerset Maugham might conjure up in one of his South East Asian novels.

*

The Brexit shock result was beginning to sink in. For internationally minded people like us, it seemed a backward step, both culturally and economically. Not only did the populist propaganda give a voice to racist and xenophobic tendencies, but I also felt it was dangerous to concentrate so much power in Britain's very centralised and antiquated political system. My experience of life in Australia left me with the impression that properly devolved and constitutional democratic power was the only effective backstop against the corrupting influence of people with too much power. I always felt that the state was not 'on your back' in Aus.

People in the UK had been promised the earth by opportunistic politicians with little sense of morality; merely cashing in on the discontent that many people felt. The wealth was clearly going, all to often, to the already well-off. This was skilfully portrayed by the dominant right-wing press as being the fault of the European Union.

Many chose to believe this assault on common sense, which fed on historical ideas of British empire and exceptionalism. Treaties were signed with no apparent intention of honouring their terms (e.g. Northern Ireland). Political 'freedom' was proclaimed to be the answer, although we had powers equal to France, with only the more populous Germany having more votes. We had more of a say than almost all the other members, but this was not enough for the British right wing ideologues, who have forever been wedded to a free market more akin to the American model (there is irony here, in that the US is itself a Federation).

145

It felt like the politics of 'Rambo' and the captains of individualism were now able to drag the rest of us down the lonely road to isolation; or so it appeared. Then the great collective effort began – with the pandemic!

Before this global tragedy we, like everyone else, were just busy getting on with our lives. We went to Sri Lanka in February and March of 2018. As usual, we had organised certain essential transfers and places to stay, whist leaving room to go 'off piste' when we felt like it. After a few days in Negombo, just north of Colombo, we visited Kandy and the tea country by train, and that was an experience like no other. The train was packed with both tourists and Sri Lankans, the vast majority of us standing or sitting sandwiched together. We were sat on our backpacks directly over the very mobile inter-carriage coupling.

All of us got on well though, and it somehow felt like fun, as we travelled through the island's beautiful countryside. The carriage doors were secured in the open position so that people could sit on the floor with their legs dangling over the edge. The windows were all flung open to provide a draught on this tropical ride.

Several times on the four-hour long journey, a Sri Lankan hawker would work his way up and then down the carriages. He was offering food, which seemed like a good idea for many. The way he balanced all his peanut based stock in his arms whilst climbing over and under us was a skill to behold. Forgive my expression here, but, to Western ears, the only way I can describe his apologies for treading on us and over us is, "Solly, velly velly solly."

Kandy was the ancient capitol of Sri Lanka and is now a World Heritage Site. It is also one of the two centres of Buddhism in the world. This is the home of the Temple of the Tooth of Gautama Buddha. As with Thai Buddhism, the

Sri Lankans seemed a peaceful people, considering their recently concluded civil war, and were patient with us Westerners.

Being at altitude and therefore cooler, the tea country felt a bit like back home. This was amplified by the British architecture and traditions. It felt a bit like little England to us at times, but we found it fascinating. For Sue, however, the highlight was definitely Galle. It was pouring down with rain when we arrived in Galle. We paid off the driver who had brought us from the wildlife park region of South Central Sri Lanka. Looking around, there was what seemed like a vacant tuk tuk (a form of three wheeled transport commonly used as local taxis in India and Sri Lanka) just next to us. Without further ado, I threw the packs in and climbed in head first, only to find a Sri Lankan popping out the other side! I was extremely apologetic, but he said it was fine and we all laughed. Only in the tropics, I thought.

We spent a few days in Galle, looking around corners and down alleys. A very interesting little place, which was often a port of call for many yachties as they made their way across the Indian Ocean.

After this we booked into a very small hotel on the beach at Thiranagama in the south-west of the country. This area was famous for its surfing and hippy vibe. Finally, we made our way up to Colombo and back to the UK. We thought Sri Lanka was a very diverse and culturally impressive place.

*

"What shall we do with it then?" asked Sue. I had received a small windfall from my old Panteg works pension. As usual I started to think about where it could take us. "Why don't we go all the way around?" I said. It was something I had always wanted to do. We had been many times half way around, going to Australia, Bali and Thailand one way, and Tahiti the other. I had thought about this quite a bit, and had worked out that jet lag would be less if we went west, not east.

Sue was, as usual, up for this venture, but there was one complication; My niece Jemma was getting married in the late December of 2018. We would need to leave in November to avoid the monsoon seasons and typhoon conditions in various places around the world. The solution was to go to India in November and then double back, attending the wedding near London, before heading west to LA and beyond.

We put all this to the STA staff in Cardiff and, as usual, they were very 'can do' about it. They were all young people but were also well travelled. They knew fellow backpacking adventurers when they saw them, even if we were two generations older than some of them! We were offered two round the world tickets which put us in the right places at the right times. So that's what we did.

First it was Goa in India (our first experience of this fascinating country), before going back to London for the wedding (which was amazing, with the bride of course looking lovely). Then, in early January, we flew West to Los Angeles for a few days before crossing the Pacific to Rarotonga in the lovely Cook Islands. This group is a protectorate of New Zealand.

Rarotonga was a contrast to LA. We had decided that, if there was a mountain on an island, we would attempt to climb it, or part of it anyway; that's what happened on Raro. One of the fascinating things about this island is that there are only two buses; one goes clockwise and the other anti-clockwise. We used the clockwise one often, as it was the shorter route to Muri beach in the South. The last bus, however, was also the clockwise one, so we usually had to go the rest of the way around to get back to our backpacker accommodation near the capitol, Avarua, in the north. Of course we didn't mind a bit. Local transport is one of the best ways to meet local people.

We spent Sue's birthday in a lagoon on Aitutaki. We were met off the plane by the 'Queen' of Aitutaki, (yes, she was a real Queen, but there are a number of them in the Cooks and they don't seem to make a fuss about it). She was hiring out one of her wooden bungalows to us for the week (the cockroaches stayed for free). She told us to get in her beat up old Toyota truck, before taking us down the road to hire a bike for us to get around on (no public transport on the island). I then followed her on the bike, to our accommodation. On the way, I couldn't help but notice that the front gardens on Aitutaki all seemed to contain graves. Apparently it is preferred to the communal system, which is used in the West; I can't see it catching on in the UK though!

By law, you have to get a local licence to drive a motor vehicle in the Cook Islands, so I turned up at the police station the next morning to see about it. Three hours later (no hurry here) the policeman turned up on his bike. All I had to do was say hello, show my (Aussie) passport, and I was given my licence. Handy for the next time!

The lagoon boat trip was wonderful. Almost no one else there, the lagoon on Aitutaki is one of the loveliest in the world. We arranged it through a man named Jones ('Jonesy' was not Welsh) who ran the Bishops family transport business. He had a hand in most things on the island, running a shop as well as his lagoon business and who knows what else. He took a shine to Sue (that happened quite often on this trip). When he picked us up from the bungalow on the morning of the lagoon trip, Jonesy insisted on taking us for a drive around the island in his mini-van. Now Aitutaki is not very big, but it was still a very nice thing to do for us (or Sue).

Among other things, we saw numerous huge trevally fish in the lagoon. As they circled us while we snorkelled, you couldn't help the feeling that *they* could eat *you* if they felt like it. We got a stamp in all four of our passports on One Foot Island and sent postcards. There is a hill at the centre of Aitutaki, so we climbed it. It was hot work in the tropical heat, but the 360degree view was well worth it.

Next it was a night flight to Auckland in New Zealand. We crossed the international dateline, so we lost Saturday the 19th of January 2019! It was, of course, much cooler out of the tropics, but after a week of relaxing and checking out Auckland, it was back across the Tropic of Capricorn and a warm welcome (talofa) in Samoa.

*

Samoa had long been on my list of places to see. I was on a bit of a mission here. We thought it would be interesting to call in at the famous Aggie Grey Hotel, overlooking Apia bay. I also wanted to visit Vailima – the Pacific homestead of Robert Louis Stevenson.

Thought to be the departure point for the settlement of the rest of Polynesia, Samoa is a unique fusion of ancient traditions and Western culture. Despite being almost entirely Christian, it still strongly embodies 'Fa'a Samoa' (the Samoan way)[15]. The tattoo (tatu) ritual is an expression of this. There are only two traditional tattooist families in Samoa; their members alone can perform these culturally important ceremonies. We witnessed one of these rituals (carried out on a woman). Once the tattooist begins the work, it must be completed, (though breaks are allowed) no matter the level of pain. The tattoo embodies and imparts information about the individual and their village and familial origins, to other Samoans.

Each village council (fono) has significant powers and responsibilities over their families and members. Where face to face negotiations fail between individuals, the fono will be referred to, and its decision is always respected by all. There is always a central village fale (building constructed of natural materials) where such meetings take place. The Samoan central authorities defer to the village councils in such local affairs.

As usual, we stayed at backpackers accommodation (with the cockroaches) but this one was special – it had a pool (still no stars though). We spent quite a lot of time in that pool. There didn't seem to be many travellers about at this time of year so it was quite peaceful.

On our first evening in the capitol, Apia, we decided to go for a walk to find some supper. The roadside drains are very large here to soak away the tropical rainfall. They are so large that I put my left foot straight through the grill of one, all the way up to the knee. Luckily nothing got damaged and I saw the funny side, *after* I had safely extracted my limb and my flip-flop.

Undeterred, we pressed on in search of some tucker. There didn't seem to be many food outlets here, but we finally decided to have a crack at an outdoor canteen type kitchen with tables under canvas to shield the diners from rain. It is usually good practice, when travelling to remote places, to eat what the locals eat. So we did. The chicken we were served was full of bones. We were told that this was normal in these parts. No one bothers to fillet chicken out here; you get all of the portion, bones and all. As ever, we were learning.

Aggie Grey's is probably unrecognisable from the way it would have been in her day. She had opened a snack bar to cater for US servicemen in 1942 and grew it progressively. She later forged links with TEAL, the flying boat forerunner of Air New Zealand. She has been written about by her friend, the writer and adventurer James Michener (himself a former US serviceman who had visited during the war). The hotel, with its romantic past, attracted film stars such as Marlon Brando and William Holden. Aggie Grey died in 1988 aged 91.

Much investment has now been put in by an international hotel chain and we enjoyed the atmosphere; of which it had plenty, whilst sipping our cups of tea (yes, even in the tropics). We also spent time checking out some of the photos and memorabilia of the hotel as it had once been. Later in our stay, we had an evening meal there.

Robert Louis Stevenson broke with convention in 1877, declaring, "A happy man or woman is a better thing to find than a five pound note." With this, he refused to take up an established profession. Hampered by a congenital lung disease, he nevertheless took an adventurous path in life. Travelling to the USA in 1877 (the journey nearly killed him), he eventually rekindled a friendship, which had commenced in a chance meeting whilst he was convalescing in France. Her name was Fanny Osborne; they grew closer and married in 1880.

Stevenson, his wife and stepson, Lloyd Osborne, eventually chartered the Casco out of San Francisco and sailed around the tropical Pacific looking for the location which best suited his health, whilst also being near to postal facilities, which were essential for his writing. It was a collaboration with the young Lloyd which produced Treasure Island, Stevenson's first major literary success, in 1883.

Eventually, after further explorations, they settled near Apia, on Upolu, the main island in modern Samoa. Here he built the home that he and his extended family lived in until his death at the age of 44. He had become immersed in local politics and spoke up for Samoa against Western exploitation. He was loved by the Samoan people, being named 'Tusitala', (teller of tales) by them. On his passing, his body was carried up nearby Mount Vaea by these grateful people, where he was laid to rest in a place he had been fond of, overlooking the sea.[16] His home, Vailima, has been lovingly cared for by the Samoans ever since.

For me, Robert Louis Stevenson's real life was as interesting as his books. He was evidently in a race against time, having been given a virtual death sentence by his doctors back in Britain. Against all the odds, he was an adventurer and that is his appeal. As with Heyerdahl, Stevenson had put himself out there.

Vailima didn't disappoint. Sue and I were moved by the privilege of visiting the great man's Samoan home. It felt almost like walking in the footsteps of a giant; the homestead was virtually as it had been when he lived and wrote in it. Afterwards, although it had begun to rain (it rains a lot in fertile Samoa), we started on the trek up Mount Vaea to see the writer's final resting place. It was a challenging climb, being slippery with the rainfall. We began to appreciate more fully the difficulty the Samoans overcame in carrying their Tusitala up this treacherous track.

At the top of Mount Vaea, Sue was wringing wet but it was more with perspiration than rain. The climb had been tough for her, but we were both glad we had done it. We spent an hour up there contemplating the precious but temporary nature of life, overlooking the northern slopes of Upolu and the sea beyond. Perhaps Stevenson had similar thoughts as he once stood on this spot; I like to think so.

On the climb down, Sue and I decided that it would be nice to cool down with a swim at the rock pool once used by RLS for the same purpose. After a little searching, we came upon the pool with its lovely little waterfall (there are many such beautiful waterfalls in Samoa). Starting to divest herself of her sodden cloths, Sue suddenly stopped, noticing that there was a big man on the far side of the pool with young children playing in the water. A skinny dip was out then!

We wrestled our clothes off, replacing them with bathers. Looking over at us, the Samoan (for that is what he was) asked, "Where are you from?" This was our first meeting with Va'aiga Tuigamala, (Inga the winger to All Black rugby fans).

He was very friendly towards us and, after hearing that we were Welsh, informed us that he was All Black number 900. "That number will always be mine," he said. We engaged in conversation, only to discover that Sue's dad had attended his All Black try scoring debut in Pontypool, South Wales. They exchanged text messages later. After a while my cover was blown; Inga said, "Steve, for a Welshman, your knowledge of rugby is appalling." I had to agree. We thought about our more rugby savvy friends (Marion and Richard), who would have loved to chat with this rugby legend. After his All Black years, Inga also played for his country of birth, Samoa.

All Black number 900 was currently running a tourist business. He asked if we would like to tour around the island with him and we said yes, straight away. The following day he met us early and we set off in his beat-up old truck to see the island. Cutting inland, we stopped at several magnificent waterfalls, in one of which we bathed (not in the buff). Just before we set off again, Inga pulled three bottles of cool drink out of the back but then realised he hadn't an opener. He just took the hasp of the seatbelt in his great hand and forced the caps off with it. On reaching the coast, we turned east and followed it around, stopping occasionally, until we were back in Apia.

During this journey, Inga told us something of his past. He went to school in New Zealand where, with a cousin, he started to go off the straight and narrow. Seeing his potential, and wanting to save him from a future of crime, his schoolmaster had a word with him. According to Inga, the following exchange took place: Va'aiga was told that he 'could be a very good sportsman' and not to 'throw it all away', that if he worked hard he could make it. Then the schoolmaster said, "I want to be the coach of the All Blacks one day, what do you want to be?" Va'aiga replied, "I want to be an All Black." They both got what they were aiming for; the schoolmaster was Graham Henry, future Wales and New Zealand rugby coach.

Inga then told us about the occasion in the 1991 competition, when the All Blacks actually 'lost' the rugby world cup (it was always presumed to be theirs to lose). Inga's wife phoned him and told the team not to come home yet. The New Zealand public were 'very annoyed' with them.

Retribution took the form of a rolling visit to schools around the country by the team members. At one school there was a competition in class to see if the children knew the nick-names of each of the players. All went well until it was Inga's turn. A little Shirley Temple look-alike put her hand up enthusiastically, calling "Miss, Miss, I know this one." Invited to share her answer with the class, the little girl said – and I quote Inga as closely as I dare – "Big B…k B…..d." When challenged about this deeply offensive remark, she said that daddy always said, "Get over the line, you Big B…k B…..d." when he looked like scoring a try. The whole team collapsed about the classroom laughing. It was months before the team let him forget it!

Inga continued to entertain us with such anecdotes about his life and rugby career. I cannot move on before imparting one final memorable story, which took place during his time playing club rugby in England. According to Inga, players can be very sensitive about their allotted places in the changing rooms. The correct hooks for their playing kits etc.

One match day Inga entered his team's changing room to prepare for the game to come. Unable to find a vacant hook on which to hang his gear, he lifted some gear off a hook and placed it on the floor. There was an audible gasp from the other players in the room, who kept their heads down. "I wouldn't do that mate," said Johnny Wilkinson. Inga took no notice and continued to change for the match. Moments later, a big South African prop-forward came into the changing room to find his kit on the floor.

"What's my kit doing on the floor," demanded the prop. Inga calmly explained that he needed the space. The South African walked up to Inga and, looking hard into his face, said in his thick South African accent, "Where I come from, we *shoot* people like you." Without flinching or missing a beat, Inga came back with, "And where I come from we *eat* people like you." Priceless!

The following day, Inga asked if we would like him to take us around parts of the island that tourists did not often go. He offered this gratis. This lovely man then took us around the western section of Upolu, stopping at various places of interest. He pointed out 'his' village on the way back. Calling into a particularly beautiful church, Inga, a devout Christian, presented a copy of his number eleven All Black shirt to Sue. It is now with Sue's dad for safe keeping.

Sadly, Inga died suddenly on the 24th of February 2022 aged just 52. We will always remember him, and 'the Samoan way', with much love and affection. Goodbye Inga. For a short but wonderful time, you were *our* Tusitala.

*

Bula! From the moment we arrived in Fiji, this traditional welcome could be heard from smiling happy faces everywhere we went. Fiji has a dark past however, being the centre of the notorious 'blackbirding' indenture scheme, whereby Governor Gordon brought Indians into Fiji to supply the demand for labour in the sugar-cane fields. You would never know that there had been a number of coups and a civil war since this beautiful country had gained independence in 1970. It was declared a Republic in 1987.[17]

We were based in backpacker accommodation on the west side of the main island, Viti Levu, near Nadi (pronounced Nandi). This was very convenient for seeing some of the wonderful Mamanuca and Yasawa islands. After a day to settle in, we took a trip around the Mamanucas' on the ferry out of the port at Denarau.

You can't avoid enjoying yourself in Fiji. We signed up with a yacht day tour to go and take a closer look at a couple of islands. We went for a snorkel at one of them, Monuriki. It has become more commonly known as 'Tom Hanks Island', as it was the set for the film Cast Away.

The Seaspray anchored about 100 metres from the beach and we were invited to jump off the boat with snorkel gear and enjoy a swim to the shore. I did, Sue went by tender. I jumped in and got a good dose of ocean up my nose! I got into difficulties as a result, and one of the crew had to throw me a life belt to stay afloat. All very embarrassing, for me that is!

We had a great on-board barbecue after, which made up for

it. We also paid a visit to a nearby island inhabited only by indigenous Fijians. We were invited to partake in the customary welcome ceremony where we imbibed the modern version of the traditional drink, Kava, ground from Yaqona root. The mouth goes a bit numb and you relax a bit, but that's all. We learned something of their way of life, which had changed very little for hundreds of years.

I had been in trouble in the water on two previous occasions (not counting my dunking in Stow Hill baths as a child); both in Thailand. The first was when we went by longtail boat to do some snorkelling near Koh Phi Phi Leh. We were open to the sea and it got choppy. I was struggling to breathe and fought my way to the longtail, pulling myself aboard with nothing more than a cut finger.

On the second occasion, I was taking my usual early morning jog along the beach in Koh Jum. I was just about to take my normal dip to cool off, before strolling back to the bungalow for a shower, followed by breakfast. For reasons which even I do not understand, I decided to swim out to a marker buoy a little way off shore. This was something I had seen others do, but by the time I got to the buoy I was getting tired. Sensing the tide was a bit against me, I immediately turned back, (the longer I was treading water, I reasoned, the more tired I would get). Finally my legs went down underneath me; I could swim no more. By some miracle, they just touched bottom. I 'walked' the rest of the way to shore. I had been lucky. There was no-one about at this hour and I could easily have drowned.

One beautiful Fijian morning we decided to go for a walk up the beach, behind our accommodation. After a short while we ambled around a small spit of dune land and there, just in front of us, was a short pontoon with a single prop float plane bobbing on the water beside it. Turtle Airways was on my hit list to look up, as they offered float plane trips over the two island groups. We had a bit of trouble finding it during the week, but there it was, very unpretentious and welcoming. We walked straight in to the office and arranged to fly as extra cargo the following day (extra, because we were not actually going to get off at one of the resort islands for a stay).

Sue and I got the float plane trip that I missed out on in Thailand. When you travel on such single engine light aircraft, weight is an issue. I saw that some of the travellers were weighing in with large luggage cases. We were told confidentially that these cases are for show; they have very little in them. Some people are strange.

The pilot was an ex-pat Kiwi by the name of Mark. We noticed that he wore no shoes, as he invited us to climb aboard – I got the co-pilots seat, brilliant. Sue was behind me and a couple were sat next to, and behind her (they were getting off at an island).

Sue got some marvellous aerial photographs of the islands (one of which I later put on the front cover of my poetry collection, 'In The Moment'). We were definitely 'in the moment'. After a short while, Sue noticed that Mark looked very still, and was slightly slumped over the controls. We had headphones on to reduce the noise, but Sue signalled to me that she thought Mark had fallen asleep, or worse!

Imagining that I might have to try and remember something from my Air Training Corps cadet days (and not worrying about it one bit), I watched Mark, noticing that the plane was not flying erratically. I decided to tell Sue that Mark was fine, but I didn't know really, until he eventually started to stir. He had to make an approach next to the island on which the other two passengers were spending a few days. On the way back, Mark swung the plane right over the nearby international runway, before 'landing' on the water and taxiing up to the pontoon. We had brought back a honeymoon couple of Brits returning from one of the islands. We all got out, having had a great experience.

The following day we did it all over again. Wonderful. A big thank you to Turtle Airways; keep it just as it is.

Later that evening, we met Mark at a nearby hotel and bought him a drink, thanking him for the flights. He said he liked his work in Fiji, but that his wife wanted to go back to live in New Zealand. We couldn't understand this at all, until we remembered Sue's homesickness in Australia.

Before we left Fiji, we took one more ferry trip around the islands. While waiting for it to arrive, we were having a cup of tea by the wharf side and noticed a very nice Island Packet 38 at anchor in the harbour. We have liked Island Packet sailing boats for years. We wondered who it might belong to. It turns out that it was almost certainly Rick Page's, author of the sailing book, 'Get Real, Get Gone' (great book Rick). He was there at about that time to shoot some film for Ben Fogle's 'New Lives in the Wild'.

Quite understandably, Fiji is used frequently by the film and TV world. On the ferry, we met a young Hawaiian who was on his way to work – on Love Island (US version). An island had been closed off for the production and he was contracted (I forget doing what) for a few months. The young man said that the work would be enough to see him through until the same time next year. Young and free; sounds very appealing. Again, we found that you meet interesting people when you travel.

*

After a week in Brisbane to cool down a bit, we travelled north to Bali. We always find the tropics heightens sensuality. This was expressed one beautiful evening on the ground floor balcony of our little retreat. It was hot and humid, with the only sounds to be heard coming from the fertile tropical life all around us. The jasmine scented garden was spread in front with bougainvilleas, frangipanis and gardenias bursting out from between the gently swaying palms. Statues of Ganesha, Shiva and the Barong watched over us. To our left was a small lotus pond with the figure of a Bodhisattva standing over it in prayer. No one was about. We were sitting in our rattan chairs out on the balcony listening to the cicadas, in full view of anyone who cared to look. We were enjoying all this with absolutely nothing on. Nature was making love all around us. It was that kind of evening.

It seemed so natural, and not at all smutty, as it would have done had we been in the repressed UK (too cold anyway). After a relaxing week in this lovely place, we went on to Kuala Lumpur and took a train up to Georgetown, near the Thai border. Then we met another Kiwi, Mark in Penang (there must be a poem in there somewhere).

We were sitting in some nice comfortable rattan chairs (outside a cafe and fully clothed this time) in the old quarter of Georgetown. We had spent the day wandering through its narrow streets, absorbing the culture, history and street art. It was late in the day and we were thinking about where to eat, when a biggish man with a briefcase came through and, on passing, asked us if we were on the 'visa run'. Now we knew what this meant from our frequent travels to Thailand.

Mark was in Penang to renew his Thai visa. You have to leave Thailand and get your passport stamped in a foreign country, before re-entering Thailand to get another visa. Permission can be granted for up to three months, depending on the reason for your stay. Penang was ideal for this, although, many travellers jump in one of the visa run minibuses, which go to the Malaysian border for this purpose.

Mark said he'd be back for a sundown drink in a few minutes, then he disappeared around the corner. Sure enough he came back and, sitting down next to me said, "It's hot as hell today." Innocently, I ordered him, and myself, a cool one (Sue didn't drink as it sometimes gave her headaches). I should have known better than to go drink for drink with a Kiwi! I didn't go drink for drink with him, but I tried. In a haze of heat and alcohol, Mark explained that he was a charter boat skipper living on his own boat with his Thai wife, near Krabi in Thailand. He'd been a police officer back in New Zealand but the work had led to a breakdown; so he got out and rebuilt his life, in the tropics.

Mark gave me his card and told us to ring the charter company and get berths on his boat when we got up to Krabi. We thought this would be a great way to wrap up our round-the-world journey. So, after a drunken so-long, this amicable antipodean left us. I sat back in a pleasant daze wondering what had just happened.

We went on by ferry to Lankawi, where we left Malaysia and crossed into Thailand via Koh Lipi (a beautiful place). We used our British passports here, as the visa is slightly longer than on the Australian ticket. Then we continued north, stopping here and there, until we arrived at Koh Jum.

*

Our beach bungalow was quite comfortable, at least the resident cat seemed to think so. We tried to discourage him, but he was usually there to welcome us when we got back at sunset each day. After about a week Sue began to notice a strange smell. I checked around but could find nothing. Sue said "It must be coming from the kitchen. Whatever they are cooking, I wish they would hurry up and get it done." But the smell (a bit like cabbage) just got worse as the days went by. I had another look around the hut and, this time, spotted a 'present', which the cat had left under the bed. We got someone in to remove the rat and clean the floor. The cat was definitely persona non grata after that!

We had decided to spend about six weeks on Koh Jum, so we hired a motorbike to get us about the island. At the northern end of Jum, there is a little beach bar called 'Peace Bar'. We found a young Brit serving behind the counter. As we supped our coconut drinks, he told us his story:

His name was Craig and he came originally from Grimsby. He'd got married and the newly-weds (barely into their twenties) had decided to move to Australia, where Craig got work on an outback station in New South Wales. Sadly, his wife did not like the life, and she left to go and live in Sydney. Craig had come to Thailand to give himself time and space to consider his future. He told us that the bar owner allowed him to sleep in the back for around £5 a night. Craig was obviously down on his luck, in both love and money. Yet he was not down in himself. He seemed to have a cheerful disposition, which, I felt, would get him through his crisis.

We both felt a little bit 'parenty', having experienced the stresses and strains of emigration ourselves. As we went back to the bike to start back down the island, I said to Sue, "I can't go from here without doing something to help." So we did. We went back and gave him enough Baht to pay his accommodation for a few weeks, or to put towards a plane ticket back to Australia (which is what we advised him to do). But for the grace of God, etc.

Time was passing all too quickly, as it usually does when you are enjoying yourself. Onto the ferry again, this time to Krabi, where we tried to get tickets for Mark's charter boat but were unsuccessful; they needed bookings of at least eight people. We spent a week in our usual backpacking accommodation, Chan-Cha-Lay, while we enjoyed the night market suppers the daytime massages and the friendly Buddhist Thai culture.

However, we did see Mark one last time. We were waiting at Krabi ferry port for our trip to Phuket and then home, when I noticed a beautiful period schooner of about sixty feet in length. Then the unmistakable figure of Mark emerged from below decks. He spotted us and immediately came ashore to shake my hand and give Sue a hug (it is always that way around).

He was sorry to hear that we couldn't get a trip on the boat. We said it was OK as we had plenty of memorable experiences to take back with us. Then it was time for him to go; he had a boat full of people to show around the islands. As he sailed away on that lovely schooner, with just a little imagination, I pictured Stevenson's Casco leaving San Francisco, bound for the South Pacific. And yes, I did write a poem about Mark; I called it 'Mark in Penang'. Cheers mate, wherever you are now.

First one way and then the other, I can safely confirm that the world is definitely round.

*

In the February of 2020 we were in Melbourne and then Sydney for a few days when we heard that Tom Hanks and his wife were 'in isolation' at a hotel in Queensland. They had contracted a virus called 'Covid-19'. As was the case for most people, we had no inkling that this thing was about to break out of China and go global. By March we were in Bali enjoying a couple of weeks at the Tamun Agung, our tropical hideaway. There was increasing media coverage in

South East Asia about the virus, by this time. We discussed it with several newly made friends. An Australian couple cut their holiday short and left on the 15th and we went on the 16th. We only just got transit through Singapore airport before it shut down. More and more countries near to China were going into 'lock-down'. Paul and Margy, two ex-pat Kiwis living in Northern Ireland, failed to get to the UK, they had to go instead to New Zealand, where they had to stay for months.

By the 24th of March, the UK was also in lock-down. So began the darkness, insecurity and loss, which has always accompanied a plague. The world went into suspended animation.

Trade Wind

Oh lovely trade wind take me far,
I wish to travel under star.
No need to enter Tardis centre,
reduce myself to plane seat renter.

With sails aloft we'll take the breeze,
the wind is fickle, sometimes a tease.
It matters not, there is no rush
we've skirted round the airport crush.

There's much to say for playing safe,
the sailors life is full of chafe.
Yet drawn to go, land problems loom,
I feel the need to leave, and soon.

Trade wind I know can sound exotic,
it is, of course, a tad quixotic.
To move away from complex matters,
where stress reduces minds to tatters.

Release and freedom there is much,
this mode of transit can give such.
Though slow and tilting it may be,
this way of life is made for me.

Trade wind will carry me through the night,
not much concern, no sense of fright.
The dark is not where fear comes by
but people, sometimes cruel and sly.

When dawn arrives, the early sky
will find me in the cockpit, lie
in slumber, there's no need to care,
the course is set, the boat knows where.

Keep your routines and your timetable,
there's life out there for those most able.
So cast out far, dull life rescind
instead, rely on fair trade wind.

Still dreaming

IX

For most people it is important to experience dreams. By dreams here, of course, I mean the kind of imaginings which humans often need in order to cope with an existence, which is perhaps unsatisfactory. As we emerge from the global darkness of disease, it seems more important than ever to convert the best of these into reality.

For many of us, dreams gradually fade to be replaced by the mundane reality of everyday life. For some of us they become reality itself, for a short while at least. For others, the dreams sometimes turn to reality, only to be replaced by still more dreams. This is how it has been for me.

From my childhood years on, I have been in thrall to dreams. When my dad brought home model aeroplane kits to build and paint with his young son, he propelled me into the struggles of World War Two. Later, I became more proficient at this hobby. While most boys of my age seemed to be in a hurry to grow up, I was somewhere else. I built models of aeroplanes, ships and even tanks, so I could 'recreate' famous battles in my back garden. The film 'The Battle of the Bulge', involving the famous tank battle, was relived this way. I had also been fascinated by Peter O'Toole's Lawrence, in David Lean's 1962 film about his adventures in World War One Arabia. Of course, I later read TE Lawrence's book, 'The Seven Pillars of Wisdom'.

This romantic version of life also surfaced when Davy Crockett paddled his raft with Huckleberry Finn down the canal on the way from junior school. Later, football provided an important diversion from the normal boyhood adolescent fantasies. Like most British boys at the time, I had my footballing idols.

I admired the 'converters' of dreams. Errol Flynn's real life, before he became a film star, was just as adventurous and exciting as his films. He was the captain of a trading boat, working around South East Asian waters. Steve McQueen was another real life adventurer. Away from films, academics like Thor Heyerdahl captured my attention with his Pacific odyssey on the Kon-Tiki.

My reading expanded my range of dreams still further, from The Swiss Family Robinson to Bernard Moitessier, the French round the world sailor. From Robert Louis Stevenson's Treasure Island and his real life adventures to Paul Theroux's 'The Great Railway Bazaar' (India) and 'The Happy Isles of Oceania' (The Pacific). Other Authors who opened up the world to me included Somerset Maugham (The Narrow Corner), Herman Melville (Typee) and Graham Green (The Quiet American).

What these authors (and many more) have in common is their ability to impart 'atmosphere'; to allow me to place myself next to the protagonist in his experience or adventure. So for me, and many others I'm sure, there is a rich vein of vicarious adventure to be tapped through literature.

As I have said throughout, I am a dreamer but, like many others, I have needed significant events in my life to crystallise dreams into action. My turbulent young romantic life brought one such moment; meeting my 'can do' wife was another. Before that, luck also had a part to play when I wasn't clever enough to study the USA in school; instead I got Australia! Similarly, I would never have made it to the land down under without my time in Panteg, where I learned a trade that was in demand there. Many, if any, of my later adventures would not have happened without these moments.

I am fortunate that my imaginings have not yet ended. I'm

still dreaming at the age of nearly sixty-nine, and looking to convert my musings into reality. In recent years (pre Covid) I developed a yen to learn to fly, so now I have both blue water and blue sky dreams! I returned to Shobdon airfield (scene of that first parachute jump) and went up for a 'taster' flight in a single engine Piper aircraft. That dream is quietly fermenting. Neither private flying nor sailing are age restricted; if you feel you can do it and you are physically capable, then you are allowed to.

Dreams have long been my ticket out, through both my imagination and my urge to see what's over the horizon; to see what it is like to convert what's inside my head into reality. For me though, thinking is still the second best way to travel. What follows is the development of my longest, unfulfilled 'stock dream'.

*

The idea first occurred to Sue in 2001, while we were on a short break to Halki, a small Greek island near Rhodes. Sitting on a beach taking in the spring sunshine, Sue noticed a sailing boat anchoring just beyond the wave line in front of us. It looked like a hired vessel, with four people on board. After securing the boat, they were in the process of climbing into the dinghy, with the clear intention of coming ashore.

"I wonder where you hire those?" asked Sue rhetorically. "No idea," I said. Sue added, "I'll go and ask them when they get ashore." This is just like Sue. If she wants to know something, she just asks! From little things, big things grow.

"From Rhodes marina," said one of the (Italian) sailors. "But you need qualifications to be allowed to hire one," he added. This got us both thinking. "We must be half-way there with our dinghy experience," said Sue. I agreed, but I knew there was more to sailing a yacht than keeping it upright (or not, in our case). "Why don't we make enquiries when we get home?" she said, so we did.

I started studying for a Royal Yachting Association (RYA) 'Day Skipper's' ticket in Cardiff yacht club. It was a theory based course and was the first step in getting the necessary qualifications to hire a sailing boat. The second step was the practical.

The means and the opportunity to take the next step came in the Autumn of 2004. Activity Holidays was a company based in the Ionian islands in Greece. They hired out sailing boats on a 'bareboat' basis (this is when you charter the boat rather as you would hire a car – you are the unsupervised skipper). They also ran a scheme in which you could learn to sail under an on-board skipper. You set up in a boat, usually with another couple, and off you went. In company with other boats, and with a lead boat in charge, the flotilla sailed around the South Ionian sea. We opted for two weeks of this 'arduous' hands-on learning; why wouldn't we? To keep the cost down, we opted for 'pot luck', which meant that we would be sharing with an unknown couple.

Ruth and David Archer were our boat buddies for a week, with another David as skipper. We hit it off with them all straight away and this was a relief, as we all had to live in a very confined space for seven days and nights. While David and I were tending to paperwork ashore, Ruth and Sue strolled along the pontoon wondering which boat we would get. They finally arrived at the end of the pontoon and there was Kronos (Greek deity of time). She looked like a tired old workhorse that had seen better days. Sue and Ruth looked at each other and laughed.

We slept in the bow, Ruth and David got the rear cabin, with David, the skipper, in the saloon on the couch (the boat was no more than 30 feet long). Later, when it rained, Kronos leaked. Sue hates leaky boats. None of us avoided a wetting. It was customary for the crew to feed the skipper, so we kept David as well fed as we were. He tried to catch fish for us all. In fact, he did more fishing than teaching! He only caught one fish. We had tuna for lunch that day.

We went from island to island, stopping every night to eat (drink) and sleep. Sometimes there would be issues with 'anchor knitting'. This is when your anchor and chain are lying under someone else's anchor and chain. There is a particular procedure for addressing this, so David and I enthusiastically followed it (with the skipper watching from the other end of the boat), and Ruth calling, "Oh God," repeatedly, as the boat, now free, slowly drifted towards a big ferry on its way out of the bay! It all sorted itself out however, and we gradually became familiar with the rudiments of boat handling.

It is regarded as a legitimate sport among boating types to sit with an 'anchor' beer, either on the boat or at a quayside bar, while observing the unfortunate antics of others who are trying to 'park' their boats. We were relaxing outside a quayside bar on the island of Kalamos one late afternoon, when one of our flotilla boats came speeding in to the (rather small) harbour. In the Med, it is conventional to park your boat by reversing it into a space at right angles to the wharf wall. Having dropped anchor at the appropriate moment as you reverse, you then make the rear of the boat fast with two lines attached to steel rings or bollards ashore. Hence, the boat is secured both fore and aft.

Anyway, this fellow flotilla member (a solicitor by the name of Sarah, as I recall) was carrying out the manoeuvre at a rate of knots. She lost control and hit a nearby boat. She was very upset and lost her rag a bit. We all knew that it was very stressful parking a boat and felt a certain sympathy for her. It *was* funny though.

We all had a memorable week and made long term friendships. On the final day, we arrived back to receive the results of our endeavours. The qualifications were 'Day Skipper non-tidal' for David and me, with 'Competent crew' for Sue and Ruth. Everyone got their tickets except me. David (the skipper) had decided that I would be ready after our second week. So it was arranged that Sue and I would take Brian, the flotilla mechanic, with us on our second week, to keep an eye on me and report back.

I didn't mind having Brian on board at all, as we both enjoyed his company; and yes, I did get my Day Skipper non-tidal ticket. On one occasion however, I was a bit preoccupied with something, and the boat was getting a bit too close to the cliffs on the North side of Ithaka. Brian casually said, "Time to put a tack in now skip?" So I did. On the plane back, we found that he'd tucked away in our bag the South Ionian chart we had been using, as a memento of our week together. If you're reading this Brian, thanks for both the tacking reminder and the chart. You meet some lovely people out there.

*

Gibraltar was where I took my Day Skipper tidal practical course. It was now June 2005 and I had just completed my RYA Yachtmaster theory course at Cardiff yacht club.

To get the Day Skipper tidal ticket, you have to take charge of a boat at night and in a tidal region. Sue and I are warm water sailors, and between the pillars of Hercules, at the entrance to the Med, is tidal. So Gibraltar it was. The week-long course went well. We had two other couples and the skipper (Chris) on board with us (it was a forty something foot Jeanneau). We went up the Spanish coast for a while, before turning south to cross the Gibraltar straits by night. The other two potential skippers (both young women) were on night skipper duties on this run.

We went to Ceuta, a Spanish enclave at the northern tip of Morocco, before going further south to Smir, in Morocco itself. We visited a souk in Tetouan. Chris, who had, himself, previously fallen at this hurdle said, "Whatever you do, don't come back with a rug." But Sue did. After spending one night and the following day in Morocco, we set off for the night time crossing back to Gib.

It was my turn to skipper, and I found it fascinating. The Gibraltar straits are among the busiest in the world. There are strict sea 'lanes' which traffic must keep to in order to avoid a collision with other boats coming into, or out of the Med. Also, there is always a strong current here, as the Atlantic continually replenishes the water evaporating from the Med. The only exception of course, is when you have to cut across; in our case, from south to north. We all had our eyes peeled for the tell-tail green, red and white lights which boats must show to indicate direction and distance. Bearing in mind that we had ships all around us, it was exciting stuff!

Again, it all went well and I gained my RYA Day Skipper certificate, Sue got her tidal Competent Crew. Now I could apply for an international licence, which is needed to charter bare-boat. We were on our way. In the Autumn, we chartered a 37-foot Jeanneau called Marut, jointly with David and Ruth. It was Turkey this time, which is another beautiful sailing area. We got off to a poor start when we gybed the boat a little bit too severely, and ripped the main sail. Once it was fixed however, we never looked back and enjoyed two wonderful weeks of sailing around the Datca peninsular.

One particularly beautiful night in a quiet bay near Mercincik has always stayed with me. We had anchored out and run the lines to shore, before cooling down in the lovely clear water. The night sky was crystal clear and the stars were out. Cold Play's X&Y album was playing on the sound system and we were laying back, each enjoying a 'cold one' after the on-board barbecue. Life felt very good.

We sailed with David and Ruth on a number of occasions after. In the Autumn of 2007 we all went to the North Ionian. It was here that David and I got into a knot when 'anchoring out' for the night at Lakka on Paxos. The safest and most comfortable way to do this is to first drop the anchor within proximity to shore (not too close, not too far away). Then, using either the dinghy or by swimming, you run a line to shore and tie it off to a suitable object (a tree is best). The person still on the boat then winches in the line until the boat is secured fore and aft.

David was in the dinghy heading towards the shore, except that he had lost one paddle over the side and was going around in circles. I was ashore, waiting to take the line from David to tie it off. Ruth was going ballistic back on the boat and Sue was cracking up. We got it sorted eventually, but not without getting sore ribs from laughing. Great fun.

Sadly, David passed away in the spring of 2022. He and Ruth had taken the next step and bought a boat, which they enjoyed for twelve years in their retirement. David loved boats and the sea. He is probably smiling now, from up there (he is definitely up there), as I relate our happy adventures together.

*

Sue and I have continued in this vein for years now. Our visits to distant places around the world complimenting our Mediterranean sailing. Sometimes we have sailed alone (bare-boating), while at other times we sail in flotilla. We have often taken Sue's Dad (he will be 89 this year) on our

Greek island adventures. Although advanced in years, he is more than capable regarding both mobility and sailing competence. I am inspired by him.

In October 2021 we went on a flotilla holiday to the South Ionian. Mr Taylor (Sue's Dad) had never been on one before, having always bare-boated with us on previous occasions. It was two weeks of fun and laughter, particularly after the 18 months of lock-downs and restrictions, which Covid-19 had brought on the world. Despite the paperwork and testing regime, we were determined to get some sailing in. So we did!

On our very first day at the marina in Sivota, a young honeymoon couple had been split off from the rest of us and were given a boat at the end of the pontoon. We wondered why, and later found out that they had tested positive for Covid! They were on that boat at the end of the pontoon for ten days, in isolation. I know a honeymoon is the time to get to know each other better, but that's going a bit far. We found out that they were OK, and the boating company (Sailing Holidays) had catered for their every need.

Sue's Dad had a wonderful time, and so did we. The flotilla was a very friendly and sociable one and we made lots of friends. The flotilla skipper was 'Yorkie'; yes, he was from there. On the third day out, going west from Kalamos to Ithaka, we saw a school of dolphins. It's always nice to see these creatures in the bow wave of the boat.

We visited many lovely places, such as Fiskardo on Kefalonia and Kioni on Ithaka. We tied up on the town quays right in amongst the chaos of restaurants and bars. It was exhilarating. On the final evening, Mr Taylor could be seen swaggering down the quayside with a lady on each arm. He had just won the 'James Bond' prize at the final group meal. He has charisma, that man! We're going again in

August (2022) and yes, Sue's dad will be with us.

*

My framing of this book has been almost entirely focussed on physical relocation; together with its associated adventures, risks, penalties and rewards. Of course, there are other, interacting, ways of securing a ticket out. For example, there is the contentment and freedom that is offered through philosophies and belief systems which centre around the inner-self; the inner-world, if you will.

I have gradually come to realise that this inner 'journey' increases in importance with the passing of time. Bali, Thailand and some Pacific islands (notably Samoa and Fiji) have found fascinating ways of absorbing Western and South Asian cultures into, or around, their own deeper belief systems. Their philosophies have, in turn, often inspired and informed other cultures. For me, there is much that the economically reductionist West can learn from such fusions.

It may be that life is about achieving a kind of wisdom through (sometimes painful) empirical experience. If that is so, reproduction aside, then I believe I have lived my share, to date. If, on the other hand, life is about finding your way through the innermost workings of the self, then perhaps I have lived a little more. I know for sure that I am still learning about life, and it continues to surprise me.

Both the inner and outer journeys are therefore now important to me, along with the sense of mortality which age brings. I hope my 'stock' around the world maritime aspiration finds expression; I haven't given up on that dream (I'll let you know if I make it). If we are to go 'blue water', Sue and I feel we must do it soon. As has often been the case in my life, however, I take a fatalistic, 'Que Sera, Sera' view. A wise man once said that you cannot escape from your future.

In the end we are, all of us, on a journey of one kind or another. Forgive me for misquoting Lawrence in David Lean's epic film:

It is written.

What remains is merely to live *It* through.

The Price of Truth and Honesty

It is better sure
to suffer through eternity,
than to concede a wrong
that victory be achieved.

To deny the prize
which is your due,
and lose what gift
lies there inside.

Let these measures act
on nature's laws,
that light be shone
on such a cause:

As Truth and Honesty.

References

(1) Arthur J. Pritchard (1957) Griffithstown...

(2) Aleksandr Solzhenitsyn (1973) The Gulag Archipelago

(3) Charlie Ward (2016) A Handful of Sand. Monash university

(4) Seumas Milne (2004) The Enemy Within

(5) Alan Bond. Wikipedia

(6) A Bold Experiment: The Trade Union Training Authority.
Wikipedia

(7) Harness History. rwwa.com.au; The Totalisator Agency Board
(TAB) of Australia

(8) Falklands War. Wikipedia

(9) The museum of Western Australia

(10) Copra – Dried coconut kernels. Wikipedia

(11) Thor Heyerdahl (1948) The Kon-Tiki Expedition: By Raft
Across the South Seas

(12) Thor Heyerdahl (1938, Eng 1974) Fatu Hiva: Back to Nature

(13) Robert Louis Stevenson (1896) In the South Seas

(14) Rock pile started by Nelson Mandela (1993) Wikipedia

(15) Fa'a Samoa, the Samoan way. Wikipedia

(16) Robert Louis Stevenson. Wikipedia

(17) Fiji. Wikipedia

Acknowledgements

My thanks go out to the people who made this book possible. To Dave Lewis, the 'can do' person in the world of Welsh publishing and pen-craft. To the many friends and workmates I have met along the way, in the UK, Australia and beyond. To my sister Julie, who shared many of the formative memories of my life. Finally, to my wife Sue, who's patience and support have been invaluable, both in the writing of the book, and the writing of much of my life.

Also by Steve

Poetry collections:

- In The Moment   2021
- In Deep   2021
- In Transit   2022

Published by
www.publishandprint.co.uk

Printed in Great Britain
by Amazon

82300210R00108